Easing Transition in Southern Africa: New Techniques for Policy Planning

Westview Replica Editions

This book is a Westview Replica Edition. The concept of
Replica Editions is a response to the crisis in academic and
informational publishing. Library budgets for books have been
severely curtailed; economic pressures on the university presses
and the few private publishing companies primarily interested in
scholarly manuscripts have severely limited the capacity of the
industry to properly serve the academic and research communities.
Many manuscripts dealing with important subjects, often representing the highest level of scholarship, are today not economically viable publishing projects. Or, if they are accepted for
publication, they are often subject to lead times ranging from
one to three years. Scholars are understandably frustrated when
they realize that their first-class research cannot be published
within a reasonable time frame, if at all.

Westview Replica Editions are our practical solution to the
problem. The concept is simple. We accept a manuscript in camera-
ready form and move it immediately into the production process.
The responsibility for textual and copy editing lies with the
author or sponsoring organization. If necessary we will advise
the author on proper preparation of footnotes and bibliography.
We prefer that the manuscript be typed according to our speci-
fications, though it may be acceptable as typed for a dissertation or prepared in some other clearly organized and readable
way. The end result is a book produced by lithography and bound
in hard covers. Initial edition sizes range from 400 to 600
copies, and a number of recent Replicas are already in second
printings. We include among Westview Replica Editions only works
of outstanding scholarly quality or of great informational value,
and we will continue to exercise our usual editorial standards
and quality control.

Easing Transition in Southern Africa:
New Techniques for Policy Planning

Charles C. Slater, Dorothy G. Jenkins,
Laszlo A. Pook, and Lee D. Dahringer

In response to the volatile political, social,
and economic situation in Southern Africa, this book
provides a new framework for the difficult task of
policy planning in times of stress and radical transition. The authors report on two complementary research methodologies--channel mapping and simulation
modeling--and their combination to form a powerful
technique for problem identification, data selection,
model formulation, and policy analysis. They describe
fully the use of channel mapping to study food systems in Lesotho (1973-1977); and the application of
simulation modeling in Rhodesia (1976-1977) to plan
for the impact of majority rule.

The late Charles C. Slater was professor of
business in the College of Business and Administration,
University of Colorado, Boulder. Dorothy G. Jenkins
is a research assistant in the Business Research
Division of the college. Laszlo A. Pook is assistant
professor of business at Colorado College. Lee D.
Dahringer is assistant professor in the School of
Business, University of North Carolina at Greensboro.

Easing Transition in Southern Africa: New Techniques for Policy Planning

Charles C. Slater, Dorothy G. Jenkins, Laszlo A. Pook, and Lee D. Dahringer

---

Westview Press / Boulder, Colorado

A Westview Replica Edition

Copyright © 1979 by Westview Press, Inc.

Published in 1979 in the United States of America by
    Westview Press, Inc.
    5500 Central Avenue
    Boulder, Colorado 80301
    Frederick A. Praeger, Publisher

Library of Congress Catalog Card Number: 79-5018
ISBN: 0-89158-481-1

Printed and bound in the United States of America

Contents

Figures

Preface

The situation in Southern Africa is volatile. The validity of statements concerning the region changes drastically with evolving circumstances, and sound research quickly becomes of historic interest only. The planning process must adapt to rapid and comprehensive transitions.

Under the leadership of Charles Slater, combined work on channel mapping and simulation modeling was developed. It was his vision that these complementary techniques could be merged to facilitate the planning process in Southern Africa. Perhaps the combined approach can help the region avoid some of the radical discontinuities that might accompany the transitions of the next decade.

This book is written for policy researchers. Details of the combined methodology are still in developmental stages and therefore a finished procedure that would be directly applicable by technicians is not yet available. The work presented is a method that can grow and change as events dictate. Channel mapping of the food system of Lesotho and simulation modeling of social process in Rhodesia are presented as prototype applications. Some of the findings may already be outdated, but the research methods remain effective and productive. The advantages of the synergistic integration of the two techniques are explored.

It is hoped that sufficient detail is presented in this book to put these techniques of channel mapping and simulation modeling and their combined application into the public domain. Perhaps other researchers and planners will use our work as a foundation for continued improvement and development. Professor Slater's role in this effort was cut short due to his death in November, 1978. However, the

Lesotho and Rhodesia projects were completed in 1977
and work on this book was started nearly a year before he died. We have simply attempted to finish
the book as he would have done.

The material on the reintegration of social
process study was the primary subject that occupied
Professor Slater's time and energy toward the end.
He considered this re-orientation of study and thought
to be a vital element in the management of the critical
issues of our time. The last section of Chapter V
represents what we gleaned from his thinking and work.

Professor Slater's valiant and uncompromising
confrontation with death was a reflection of his
life: he continued to learn, and teach, and write,
to the very end. He truly cared about the people
of the world, and we will miss him as a colleague,
innovative thinker, and friend.

We dedicate this book to Professor Slater's
beloved family, Emma, Steven and Ellen: how much
they lost we will never know, what he gave us we
will never forget.

Dori Jenkins, Business Research Division,
  University of Colorado, Boulder
Lee Dahringer, University of North Carolina at
  Greensboro
Laci Pook, Colorado College, Colorado Springs

Acknowledgments

Originally we thought that perhaps we could omit this section. Acknowledgments always sound so strained, and they often seem to be no more than obligated and passing references to friends. However, so many generous people helped us in the preparation of this book that we cannot ignore their contribution.

Phil White and Claude McMillan of the University of Colorado College of Business Administration supplied invaluable encouragement, particularly in the difficult period just after Professor Slater's death. The Business Research Division at C.U. provided a work space and generous staff support. For this we are especially grateful to Charles Goeldner and Gloria Day. Charles Howe of the University of Colorado Economics Department provided useful editorial review. Our research on data sources was greatly aided by Marion Doro of Connecticut College, Moore Crossey of the Yale University Library Africana Collection, and Daniel Britz of the Library of African Studies at Northwestern University.

The United States Agency for International Development generously provided financial support for both the Lesotho channel mapping and the Rhodesian simulation project. In addition, Rogers Cannell then of Louis Berger International, Stan Wellisz of Columbia University, Geoffrey Walsham of Cambridge University, and Paul Talmey of the University of Colorado provided substantive guidance on the Rhodesian project. Also, the staff of Planning Assistance Inc., especially Charles Patterson and their entire support team in Lesotho, contributed immensely to the success of the channel mapping project.

Ruby Fulk's editing and typing skill saved us from many of our own mistakes. We thank the College of Business and Economics of Colorado College for the financial support of manuscript preparation.

We are especially grateful to Geoff Sanders of
the University of Colorado Economics Department.
He performed diligent service as an outside reader
and asked many exacting questions about the content
of the book. His suggestions were the source of
significant improvements.

In the final analysis, of course, responsibility
for the book is our own, but we are indebted to those
people who helped us achieve that responsibility.

I. Easing Transition: An Overview of Methodologies

This book reports on two different research and planning projects: a general systems simulation model of Rhodesia developed in 1976 and 1977, and a nutrition and food systems channel mapping of the Kingdom of Lesotho developed from 1975 through 1977. Individually these studies are relevant to the planning for development and transition to majority rule in Southern Africa, but combined as a new approach to the planning of social and economic change, they may be of considerable significance.

The objective of this book is to provide detailed knowledge of these new techniques and their application to currently serious problems in Southern Africa. It is not our intent to develop a total survey of the history of the problems of the region, but only to position this work in relation to the development and integration tasks facing most of the nations in Southern Africa.

The development problems facing Southern Africa are unique, complex, and rapidly evolving. Political forces and economic potentials lead now to the redistribution of roles. Since the path of change is likely to be uneven, some new techniques may prove very useful in describing the socio-economic system and assessing trade-offs among the many interested parties in this rich, but troubled, region. Most readers are, no doubt, familiar with the economic history of the region. Indeed, many readers may be more familiar with the broad sweep of history and current problems than are the writers. However, our task is only to position the two research and planning programs, and not to recite all the events leading to the apparent need for new planning and development techniques.

Over the past two and half centuries, several relatively independent and technologically primitive African societies experienced the arrival of Europeans in their lands. The Europeans were technologically more sophisticated than the Africans whose lands they invaded. The colonial societies assigned very limited roles to the Africans, not only in technical tasks, but also in the political and economic activity of the region. In Rhodesia, this pattern has continued until 1979, with expectation of change in the near future.

The kingdom of Lesotho has always been independent, but it was a British Trust Territory from 1875 to 1966. Although Lesotho's political independence has not been in question for most of this century, its economic dependence upon the Republic of South Africa is a necessary but constraining force on development.

The problems of the former Trust Territories - Botswana, Swaziland, and Lesotho - may be somewhat different than the problems of transition for communities that have been fully colonial in their status - Rhodesia, Namibia, Mozambique, and the Republic of South Africa. The political leadership and managerial approaches brought to fully colonial nations by the Europeans have not, to date, been fully transferred to African hands. As a result, dualistic economies operate with limited expectations that the neo-colonial system can become a post colonial community without difficult structural change.

The power structure is important to understanding the dynamics of policy formation and change. Historically few societies have been willing to demand significant changes in structure, but Southern Africa is at a crossroads of change. The power structure in a society is directly related to income distribution. The elite, rarely more than one or two percent of the population, control the resources and the political and military power. The praetorian guards are public officials who have a vested interest in maintaining the status quo, but are not really in power. The upper middle class consists of professionals and merchants. In industrial nations, this class is growing rapidly but in less developed countries, it is almost non-existent. The lower middle class is the working class and it has a greater percentage of the population in industrial nations than in less developed nations also. The lower class consists of subsistence farmers and traditionalists in less developed nations, and transfer recipients in industrial nations. In any society, the dominant

2

elite wants to stay in power as its first goal.
Therefore enough income will be distributed to avoid
conflict, but security may be emphasized to the ex-
clusion of life support for some citizens. In
Southern Africa, demands for radical change are growing louder and shifts in the distribution of power
seem inevitable. The needs for development and transition to greater African participation in the
governance and economic opportunities of Southern
Africa are different in each of the nations and
territories, but the information base and the mechanisms for assessing trade-offs are similar.

New Approaches to Planning

One of the problems facing Southern African
nations is the development of new goals for economic
growth and employment, income distribution, and
political processes. Ideally these new goals will
accommodate all the residents, African, Coloured,
Asian and European, in an evolutionary process leading toward equalization of opportunity without vio-
lence or loss of technical capability and output.
However, the choice of development strategies should
be internally determined rather than externally
imposed. The people of the region must make their
own decisions. The research and planning programs
offered here may help in these important decisions,
and they should become available to all interested
parties. Hopefully, this monograph will help serve
this process of dissemination. Even if the programs
described here are not immediately utilized and expanded in application, this work may stimulate
interest and encourage the development of other related approaches.
Simulation modeling and channel mapping, as
complementary approaches in planning, have had
limited and largely separate applications in Africa
and elsewhere. It is hoped that this monograph can
present a new synthesis that will strengthen the
development planning process particularly where harsh
political and economic trade-offs must be weighed.
Before presenting the specific details of the
methodologies and results of the food systems study
of Lesotho and the simulation assessment of trade-
offs in the transition to majority rule in Rhodesia,
it is useful to provide readers with a road map of the
two methodologies and to outline the merging of the
two into a totally new process for planning development and transition.

3

The Food System and Nutritional Performance in Lesotho

On a per capita basis, Lesotho is one of the most heavily food aid dependent nations in the world, with about one tenth of all food supplied by aid donors. In addition, Lesotho imports about 40 percent of its food needs from the Republic of South Africa, usually in finished forms such as maize meal, dry beans, and other processed foods. In turn, Lesotho exports the labor services of miners. About three fifths of the male work force is employed in the Republic of South Africa on contracts of varying duration.

Because of suspected infant malnutrition and some nutritional problems among older people, there was concern in Lesotho about the adequacy of the food supply. Moreover the possibility that the number of miners working in the R.S.A. might be reduced was a threat to Lesotho's available income for the purchase of foods. Thus a short term as well as a possible long term food and nutrition problem was suspected in 1975. Recognition of this vulnerability led the United States Agency for International Development (U.S.A.I.D.) to support a national nutrition planning conference. The Conference was held in December, 1975.

The Lesotho National Nutrition Conference was held at the Roma campus of The National University of Lesotho and was attended by representatives of the several government ministries and agencies concerned with food and nutrition. In addition, the voluntary agencies and donor assistance agencies of other nations were in attendance. Planning Assistance Inc., a voluntary agency concerned with development planning, was co-ordinator of the three-day conference. The impact of the Conference was to gain recognition of the nutrition problem in Lesotho and to encourage cooperation among the agencies involved. The actions taken were two. First, a fact finding study of nutritional status and prospects was initiated. That effort is reported here. A second action was the formation of an inter-ministerial Food and Nutrition Council. Together these actions go a long way to assuring careful attention to future nutrition needs of the nation. At this writing, the first generation of Food Systems Research Studies has been completed. With some delays, the Lesotho Food and Nutrition Council is formed and operating to implement some of the suggestions from the first research as well as exploring ways to sustain the research monitoring of the food system.

As the next chapter will describe, the food system research study utilized a variety of research techniques: anthropometry to assess the performance of the food system for children, survey research of households as consumers and farmers, as well as marketing and economic research methods to study food production and trade channels. These methodologies were different from the techniques of research applied in the economic simulation of the Rhodesian economy.

The Rhodesian General Systems Simulation

The Southern African Task Force of U.S.A.I.D. learned of the simulation model of the Kenyan economy, that Slater and Walsham had developed [26], and asked our group to develop a similar model of the Rhodesian economy to assess the impact on that economy of various scenarios of non-violent transition to majority rule. The modeling of Rhodesia involved only slight modifications of the Kenyan model structure; specifically the addition of a mining sector, output constraints, and a measure to reflect emigration of households.

The model, called ZIMSIM (for Zimbabwian simulation), allowed us to examine several probable economic and social changes. The work on structuring and parameterizing required about two months, from mid-December, 1976 through early February, 1977. Reports were then prepared for U.S.A.I.D. over the first half of 1977. Clearance for publication of the preliminary results and further development was obtained from U.S.A.I.D. in December, 1977.*

The Rhodesian model closely follows the structure and processing features of the model of Kenya. In this case, there was limited opportunity to validate the simulation by checking output against the performance of the economy. Thus what is presented here is recognized to be a feasible method for comparative policy analysis and not a fully validated and tested model. The third chapter and the appendix material present the details of this work.

Integration of Channel Mapping and DIOSIM Modeling

The evolution of these two complementary techniques for development planning occurred over the past ten years. In an effort to better understand the role

---

*Thomas H. E. Quimby, Director of the Office of Southern African Affairs wrote a letter of release, dated December 22, 1977.

of marketing and distribution in the development
process as well as explore the impact of modernization of food marketing channels upon development, a
series of studies was conducted in Latin America from
1964 through 1969 [18, 19, 21, 23]. A limited simulation method was developed in these studies in Bolivia
and Brazil. It was a simulation method designed
initially to assess trade-offs between food marketing
modernization and the displacement of labor employed
but under-utilized in the traditional food marketing
system.

The effort to improve the simulation to more fully
describe economic and social process of development was
resumed in a new setting and with a broader perspective
in 1972. Slater worked in Kenya with the Ford Foundation as an economic advisor to the Ministry of Finance
and Planning. Trade-offs among goals of sector growth,
household income, distribution of that income, employment by sector and technical level and many similar
issues were faced in the process of assisting with
the drafting of the 1974-78 Five Year Development
Plan for Kenya.

The modeling concepts of KENSIM were developed
by Slater and Walsham in Kenya [26]. They were later
joined in this work by Mahendra Shah, Chairman of the
Electrical Engineering Department at Nairobi University. The KENSIM modeling concepts have now been
applied in several other projects: ZIMSIM [27],
COLOSIM [20], and USSIM [16]. COLOSIM is a simulation
of the economy of the state of Colorado developed in
1977 and 1978 for the Office of the Governor to assess
the impact of drought and now applied to other problems
of state Government planning [22]. USSIM is an unpublished prototype model of the United States economy.
It has been parameterized only from 1960 to 1970 and
its principal use has been to test the reliability
and sensitivity of the model concepts. One major
development of USSIM has been the design of new sensitivity testing concepts by Laszlo Pook reported in
his dissertation [16]. The testing methodology is
applicable to large scale mathematical models in general.

The modeling work has now converged again with
channel mapping studies of basic life support systems.
The study of the food system of Lesotho has been
explored as a research technique complementary to the
trade-off assessment simulation modeling in Rhodesia.
Chapter IV will discuss the requirements and potential
gains from an integrated study of development planning
involving mapping of the basic life support systems
and the use of these mappings as guidance for

6

parameterizing the general systems simulation model.

Open systems models, or channel mappings, can be developed of the systems which provide each of the life support priorities. These models can give careful consideration to the corresponding aspects of life fulfillment activities. As in the case of the Lesotho food study, base levels of adequacy can be established and tested by objective criteria. The objective standard may be difficult to determine in cases where quality of life issues seem inseparable from life support issues: a corrugated squatter's shack may provide shelter, but it probably does not fulfill the requirements of adequate housing. Therefore, in some instances, the standard may have to be based more closely upon expectations within the society, but some estimate of adequacy can be determined. The delivery system can then be judged against that standard. A series of such open systems models can provide a socioeconomic overview of the society.

The open system models and evaluation of service in each area will lead to suggestions for changes and improvements. However, comprehensive evaluation of these suggestions will necessitate closed systems simulation models. As in the case of market modernization in Latin America, some of the policies suggested by single sector open system analysis might prove to have overwhelming negative secondary impacts. Simulation modeling of the entire system can evaluate the policies generated by channel mapping in terms of other channels and concomitant changes in them. In this way, simulation can add a practical dimension to the policy derived from channel mapping research.

Channel mapping can also contribute directly to the value of simulation modeling. The information gathered by channel mapping can be used to refine the parameter estimates of the DIOSIM model. Without such mapping, data sources are usually limited to the input/output table of the region modeled, national income accounts, and household budget surveys. The data generated by the channel mapping can be used to complement these other sources and also to verify their reliability. In addition, channel mapping data can be used to verify the output of the model during the years in which the model is calibrated. Finally, channel mapping can help to define the scenarios and choose policy options. Without a full understanding of the channels, policies may be examined that are not the most critical at a given time.

Channel mapping and simulation modeling are both presented as aids to the planning process. The planning process frequently occurs with little systematic linkage

7

between sector plans and trade-off assessment, and
with little attention to broadening the base of
participation in decision-making. In many communities, sector planning is done entirely within the
sector and trade-offs are assessed in a much simpler
manner. Figure 1.1 shows the rudimentary process of
development planning. It is important to note the
absence of any formal assessment of priority preferences and the lack of an explicit method to assess
trade-offs. This process limits the community's
ability to conduct dialogues on the development
strategies chosen. It also enables the political
elite to ignore the overall welfare results of various
plans and thus diminishes the value of welfare goals.

Figure 1.1   Rudimentary Process of Development
             Planning

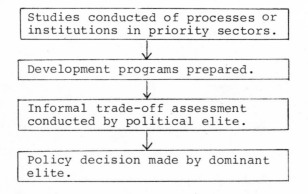

Presently there is much criticism of the research done to assist in the decision process. On
one hand, systems scientists concerned with simulation and economic modeling are criticized for lack
of relevance in their designs. Some see their work
as too esoteric and lacking in practical detail. On
the other hand, the sector study specialists are
criticized for a lack of concern for the trade-offs
and secondary impacts associated with a simple minded
effort to "sell" their project. There seems to be
some validity to both sets of charges. The separate
approach of both sector expanding projects and high
technology systems modeling is less effective than
more coordinated work would be, and a co-ordinated
effort could answer both of these criticisms.

Almost any sector enhancing project will benefit the sector participants differently. But the
trade-offs are usually ignored. For example, the
transfer of technology from industrial to developing
communities often ignores employment and income distribution consequences of the use of tractors rather
than hand labor. Technological change in the indus-
trialized society moved jobs from farm to factory.
In the less developed countries, the job usually
leaves the nation for the tractor factory and fuel
producing nations. Thus trade-off assessment is
crucial to good decisions. By positioning sector
development programs in a DIOSIM model of the economy,
these trade-offs become apparent.

The design of simulations and macro econometric
models rarely calls for an iterative and interactive
generation process. Instead, many designers complain
of the poor quality of data. The improvement of
sector definition, parameter estimation, and scenario
planning could follow from the interaction of sector
descriptive research and model design. Regrettably,
such cooperative work is rare. This stems from the
fact that the sector research client is usually a sub-
sector of the life support system and maximization of
the sub-sector status is the client's goal rather than
the optimization of the total life support system. In
contrast, the macro system client is often a central
bank or financial planning institution. In this case,
the perceived tools of intervention are monetary and
occasionally fiscal policy. Detailed performance of
major sectors of the life support system are rarely
seen as useful information.

Many policy options grow out of sectoral development plans, but they need to be evaluated in terms of
growth, employment, income distribution, and resource
utilization. Thus a reliable simulation model that
reports on growth by sector; employment by sector and
income/demographic group; income distribution by
demographic group; resource utilization by sector and
household group; and taxes by sector and household
groups; provides a method for assessing policy options
in terms of overall trade-offs.

Many groups within the government as well as the
society in general will benefit from the integration
of channel mapping and simulation modeling techniques.
In the central government, this integration would provide a clearer definition of goals and better communication between the Prime Minister's staff and the
Ministries of Finance and Planning, Agriculture,
Commerce and Industry, and Health. Coordination of
the two research methods would help to provide the

basis for ministerial communication and cooperation. In addition, the integration would provide clearer guidelines and more complete information to regional and local planners. Industry groups could work more effectively with a more direct statement of government goals. The combined analysis of channel mapping and simulation modeling could also help industry to derive effective goals and policies within each processing sector. The scope and direction of foreign aid could also be targeted more efficiently based on this new level of information. Perhaps more importantly, or as a sum of these other effects, citizens in life roles would benefit from the welfare results of more effective policy planning.

It is the objective of this book to present a new integrated method of studying socio-economic change as well as the consequences of policies designed to respond to change. The fourth chapter will provide a description of how the two complementary planning techniques, channel mapping and simulation modeling, can be combined and utilized for both project planning and trade-off assessment for an overall development strategy.

Finally the last chapter will present some conclusions and new perspectives. It will begin with a discussion of two classifications of social science research modes. Next some general conclusions about channel mapping and simulation modeling will be reviewed. Then the discussion will turn to some suggested improvements in the techniques and further applications. The book will conclude with a discussion of the integration of social process study and the role that these techniques could play in that re-orientation.

These new methods are techniques for describing a social system (Lesotho work) and assessing trade-offs (Rhodesia work). In that sense they are politically neutral methodologies. They could be applied by governments of any persuasion, capitalist, Keynesian, or Marxist. As research analysts, we are providing policy tools for business (local or international) and government. We hope to remain policy neutral, although each of us as authors has specific hopes for the direction of governing policy and the breadth of participation in the societies of Southern Africa.

It is our belief that the availability of improved methods for study of these complex societies can facilitate a peaceful transition that is beneficial for all citizens.

II. Life Support Systems Mapping: The Food System of Lesotho

     This chapter describes a methodology for deriving a description of the life support systems of communities. The case presented here will be a study of the food system of Lesotho, but the methodology could be generalized to other support systems in other Southern African communities. The method consists of complete channel mapping so that the system is described from the initial inputs to end use. It renders a closed system description that is both comprehensive and detailed.

     This methodology provides a description that can be invaluable in the policy making process. It provides information that is particularly critical when policy formation is constrained by the type of severe tensions that currently characterize Southern Africa. Complete channel mapping provides a firm data base for the policy formation function by evaluating the situation which exists and analyzing the extent and location of problems. Thus channel mapping suggests points of intervention and possible strategies for improvement. Most policies require evaluation in terms of a broad range of factors to determine their feasibility. Strategies to implement policy also require similar rigorous examination. A firm data base, in the form of a comprehensive description, can facilitate this type of analysis. In addition, this data base is complementary to the trade-off assessment methodology that is presented in Chapter III. If the description of the system is complete, the parameterization of the simulation model will be more accurate and the effects of alternative policies will be more evident.

     This chapter discusses three major topics: general methods of channel mapping, the Lesotho case, and generalization to other life support systems and other communities. The section on general methodology will discuss the theory and procedures of channel mapping.

The next section will present Lesotho as a case study of the application of this methodology. It will begin with a general description of the nation of Lesotho and then discuss nutrition history in Lesotho and the background of this project. This discussion will emphasize the importance of collaborative planning. Then the methodology as applied in Lesotho will be presented, including a description of the survey instruments, institutionalization of the research capability, sample design, and anthropometry as an objective measure of food system performance. The results and general conclusions about the food system, as derived by this method, are then presented. The section on Lesotho as a case study concludes with a discussion of the types of strategies for enhancing the performance of the food system that this analysis suggests. This discussion includes how the strategies derive from this descriptive methodology, a discussion of inappropriate vs. appropriate technology, and examples of actual strategies.

The final section of Chapter II discusses the motivation and methods for adapting this channel mapping methodology to other communities and other life support systems. Lesotho is presented only as a case study of this methodology and this final section emphasizes this context. The value of other applications is outlined and continued uses are suggested.

Methodology for Descriptive Research Into Life Support Systems

The methodology and framework described here will concern the food system, because food and nutrition are critical to the performance of any community. But the channel mapping methodology could also be applied to other sectors of the economy.

The intention of food channel mapping is to investigate and provide a complete description of the food system, from production through processing and distribution to consumption. Surveys of channel participants are conducted at each level and the results of these surveys are integrated to provide a closed system description of the entire sector. Objective measures of system performance are taken and these measures are assessed in conjunction with the description to give an evaluation of how the food system is performing in relation to channel participants.

12

The essential element of the channel mapping technique is surveys of channel participants at all levels. For a food system study, this includes industrial organization studies of imported and internally produced foods, consumer surveys, retailer surveys and surveys which establish an objective criteria of performance.

Industrial organization studies are the most formal of these surveys: they have had the most detailed precedent in the literature. They trace the flow of food from production on commercial farms, through processing. They also evaluate the channels through which food imports flow. The organization and practices of individual firms, and the economic and nutritional results which emerge, are subjected to detailed scrutiny. In the aggregate, industrial organization studies provide a description of the organization, practices, and performance of the entire industry.

In industrial nations, these studies are complex and numerous studies of individual firms are necessary to provide the overall description of the industry. In developing countries, the number of firms participating in the food industry is more limited and generally an even smaller number control most of the industry. The firms which are crucial to the analysis can usually be determined by studying food products in the national statistics.

Consumer surveys involve questions about households, subsistence farming and shopping behavior. Some of the information sought is demographics. One of the most critical aspects of consumer surveys is to determine the income patterns of households, because these patterns affect all other consumer behavior. The income generating sources of households include rents, wages, transfers, and income in kind from the traditional sector. It is important to distinguish between these sources and also to determine the relative importance of each. Self-report measures tend to be somewhat inaccurate, but nonetheless they are an essential source of information. The income application of households is equally critical. Households acquire and consume goods and services from both the commercial and traditional sectors. The types and amounts of these purchases should be determined, with particular attention to the product of specific interest; in this case, food. Households also spend money on taxes to purchase government services, save money, and make transfers to extended families. The extent and frequency of these expenditures should be investigated.

13

Consumer surveys seek to delineate the consumers' interaction with the commercial channel and also his dependence on traditional agriculture as a source of food. Consumer attitudes, perceived problems, and satisfaction regarding the existing food system should be evaluated as possible sources of information concerning how well the consumer is served by the existing food system. Consumer surveys can exhibit a significant range of variation in design, but they should attempt to thoroughly investigate all aspects of consumption behavior that relate to the channel being considered.

Trade channel surveys trace the links between the producer and the consumer. In the case of the food system, trader surveys should cover retail establishments including cafes, general dealers, butchers, bakers, grocers, peddlers, and green grocers. Any commercial outlet that sells food may be considered. In almost any country, the number of these establishments will prohibit a complete survey of each one. Usually government statistics and census data can be used to establish a representative sample by region and type of establishment. Trade surveys should seek to determine the selection of products available and price levels. It should also investigate the convenience of location to households of the retail outlets. Regional differences in selection, price and convenience of location should be noted. As in the consumer survey, questions about perceived risks, problems faced, and sources of loss will provide useful information concerning the performance at this level of the channel.

The final essential survey is one that uses objective criteria to evaluate the performance of the food system. For children, anthropometry may be used to evaluate their nutritional status against model groups. Anthropometry can be used to give estimates of chronic and acute undernutrition, and it can help define groups that are in high risk situations. The results derived for children can be used as an indicator of the overall nutritional status of the community. However, specific measures for other age groups and population segments are needed to provide more exacting evaluation. The issue of middle class nutritional status, particularly in industrial nations, is complicated and evaluation is imprecise because of a lack of consensus on a standard performance measure. The use of this objective criteria survey can provide an estimate of the extent to which malnutrition is a problem for the community and it can also help to identify the particularly vulnerable groups.

14

After the survey instruments have been designed to derive maximum information, they should be translated into the local language and piloted. Frequently the pilot studies will reveal language difficulties, areas of information that are not thorough enough, and new areas that need investigation. The pilot studies can lead to useful revision of the surveys and thus this phase of the research should be undertaken with thoroughness and precision.

The sample frames for these different surveys will vary. The industrial organization survey can frequently reach all of the major producers and importers of food, because channel participants at this level are limited in number. Government tax statistics will usually delineate the crucial firms. The consumer surveys and the nutritional status survey should have similar, if not identical, sample frames. Random sample in census enumeration areas, with adjustment made for population density, will generally provide a representative sample. This sample is best designed by the staff of the census bureau. The sample for the retailer survey should be balanced for regional and type of store representation.

When the sample frames have been drawn and the survey instruments have been tested and refined, the surveys should be conducted and the data analyzed. This phase of the research should occur as rapidly as possible to minimize seasonal differences in food intake. The analysis of the data should include integration into a closed system view of the food system. Sources and amounts of food supply and demand should be compared and analyzed. Analysis of channel participants' problems and shortfalls in supply should suggest possible policies to alleviate the inadequacies and enhance the performance of the system.

In conclusion, this channel mapping methodology is positive, descriptive research with a policy orientation. Throughout the project, the perspective must be maintained of trying to develop a comprehensive, integrated view of the food system that is detailed enough to provide information at many levels along the channel. With this orientation, the research will be able to facilitate the policy formation process.

Lesotho as a Case Study

The preceding section presented a brief description of the channel mapping technique. Elements of the research were outlined and goals and outcomes were discussed. But the most effective way to illustrate a research methodology is to describe its

application to a case study. Therefore this section
will present the food system study of Lesotho as
an application of complete channel mapping. First,
a general description and history of Lesotho will be
presented, and then a brief statement of current
economic performance will be given. Next the nutrition history of Lesotho and the background of this
project will be discussed. The methodology as applied
to Lesotho will then be described including a description of results and conclusions. Finally, the
strategies for enhancement as developed by this study
will be outlined.

Lesotho is a tiny nation (30,300 square kilometers),
similar in size to Belgium and slightly larger than the
American state of Maryland. It is completely surrounded
by the provinces of the Republic of South Africa;
the Orange Free State on the west and north, Natal
and the Transkei on the east, and Cape Province on
the south. It is one hundred and fifty miles across
the rugged and undeveloped Transkei to the Indian
Ocean.

The geography of Lesotho is mountainous: it is
the only nation in the world entirely above one
thousand meters. The eastern three quarters of the
country is covered by the rugged and largely in-
accessible Maloti Mountains and the western quarter
is lowlands. The country is geographically divided
into three distinct regions: the lowlands, the foothills, and the mountains. The lowlands contain the
urban areas, most of the population, government head-
quarters, and the best agricultural land. In the
foothills and the mountains, there is limited farming, herding and grazing, and a very sparse population. The climate varies regionally, but all areas
are subject to severe drought. Only 13 percent of
the land is arable and the topography and the intense
rains which end droughts make the land naturally
susceptible to erosion [3, p. 5].

The Basotho nation first coalesced under the
rule of Moshoeshoe I during the 1820s at the mountain
fortress of Thaba-Bosiu. This vantage was success-
fully defended against the Zulu, the Amangwane, the
Boers, and the British. Lesotho became a British
protectorate in 1884 and the wars which had plagued
its entire history ceased.

By the end of the 19th century, Lesotho was a
veritable wheat bowl, exporting large harvests of
grain to the boom mining towns in South Africa. But
peace and British medicine caused a rapid increase in
population: between 1891 and 1904 the nation
experienced a population growth of 30 percent.

The pressures of population strained the land. Less
land was allowed to lay fallow and soil quality
deteriorated from over-use.

In 1932, world depression and severe drought
worsened Lesotho's condition. The wool and mohair
markets collapsed. Drought destroyed crops and livestock, and many people died of starvation. The rains
which ended the drought carved deep gullies in the
over-cropped land. Farmers were driven to the foothills in search of land, but this trend only contributed to the problems of erosion. Declining acreage
and crop yields, forced more Basotho to seek employment in the mines of the Republic of South Africa.

Lesotho struggled in this economic and social
condition until independence in 1966. The salient
characteristics of a free Lesotho read like a development disaster: staggering overpopulation, lack of
manpower due to migrant labor, overwhelming problems
of erosion, and virtually no industry nor socio-economic
infrastructure.

The 1976 census reported that Lesotho had a
population of 1,210,906, with an annual growth rate
roughly equivalent to the population of Maseru.
Population density varies, but with 94 percent of the
population in the lowlands, this region has one of the
highest population densities in all of rural Africa.
Some rural households do not have land to cultivate.

Lesotho is one of the poorest nations in the
world. The gross domestic product was on the order
of R70 million in 1974-75, approximately one half
of migrant laborers' wages in the Republic of South
Africa [3, p. 6]. Agriculture is the primary con-
tributor to the GDP, but even so approximately 11 percent of the food consumed is from donated sources.
The distribution of income is remarkably egalitarian,
largely because of the land tenure system and the
wide spread effect of miners' remittances. However,
this equality of income simply means that everyone
is equally poor.

The essential economic and political fact in
Lesotho is dependence on the Republic of South Africa.
When the British granted independence to Lesotho,
the R.S.A. sought to strengthen the ties of economic
dependence. The ties were already established in that
more than one-half of the male labor force worked in
the R.S.A., and Lesotho is landlocked by Republic
provinces so all transportation of imports and exports
is essentially dependent. The dependence caused by
migrant labor patterns has grave social consequences
and serious political implications for Lesotho. It
is the source of long term insecurity. It has been

17

said that "the most important structural characteristic of Southern Africa is the virtually unchallenged
economic domination of the R.S.A." [5, p. 29].

The economic dependence of Lesotho on the Republic of South Africa is reflected in the nation's
membership in the South African Customs Union. Other
members of the Union are Swaziland, Botswana, and the
R.S.A. The rand is the common monetary unit of these
nations. (In 1976, one rand equalled 1.15 dollars
American.) All customs, excise and sales taxes are
paid to a common pool, and Lesotho's share of the
revenue is based on the value of its imports. Lesotho's annual revenue from this source amounts to
approximately one-half of the total government of
Lesotho revenue [9, p. 61]. This revenue is a significant membership benefit to Lesotho, as is free
access to the R.S.A. market which has considerable
purchasing power. However, the Customs Union has the
distinct disadvantage of putting the R.S.A. essentially in control of Lesotho's economy. Lesotho bears
the burden of the price raising effects of protective
tariffs, loss of fiscal discretion (because of the
common monetary unit) and the polarization of development [3, p. 5]. Lesotho's economic position has been
summed up by World Bank analysis as follows, "The
maneuverability of the government of Lesotho in its
economic policies is severely hampered by the country's
close ties with South Africa" [29, p. 3].

Lesotho's dependence on the R.S.A. is presently
an economic necessity. The dependence forms the
bulwark of Lesotho's financial stability. However,
the detrimental effects of such complete reliance are
reflected in the re-inforcing cycle that is established by the migrant labor practices. With less
skilled labor at home, it is difficult for Lesotho
to develop a strong resource base in either agriculture or industry. Therefore, more of her people must
seek work in the Republic of South Africa. This
cycle of dependence and economic control directly
affects the performance of the food system of Lesotho
and policies concerning it.

Nutrition History and Background of this Project -
Population pressure, diminishing crop yields, erosion,
drought, crop failure, and deteriorating soil have
plagued the food system of Lesotho since the beginning
of this century. The Basotho were exporters of food.
They became importers; victims of world prices and
drought cycles, and dependent upon money flows from
the R.S.A. In a nation so strained, nutritional
adequacy is difficult to provide. Pellagra, scurvy,
and kwashiorkor became symptoms of a diet composed

18

primarily of maize where there was not enough of it!

In order to evaluate the nutritional status of the Basotho, the World Health Organization conducted a survey from 1956 through 1960 [13]. The study found that the Basotho diet was deficient in calories, protein, vitamin A, riboflavin, niacin, calcium and iodine. Thirty percent of the children were found to be underweight. Fifteen percent of the population evidenced pellagra during the summer season and 15 percent had obvious goiter. Under recommendation of the WHO study, a government coordinating office, the Permanent Bureau of Nutrition, was established. It was the responsibility of this office to coordinate a series of target projects, but the office had no direct links to policy makers. The projects conducted led to some improvement in nutritional status, but did not provide an integrated, comprehensive approach to the problem of Basotho nutrition.

In 1975, recognition of the existing shortfalls and potential future dangers motivated the government of Lesotho to call a Conference to evaluate the nutrition situation in the country and to plan improvements. This Conference was supported by the United States Agency for International Development. Planning Assistance, a non-profit agency based in New York City, was contracted to coordinate the effort. The concept of collaborative planning was stressed throughout the project: each country must do nutrition planning on an individual basis and all interested parties should be involved from the inception of the planning process.

The Lesotho National Nutrition Conference was held in December 1975. The Conference lasted for two and one-half days and was attended by about one hundred high level government ministry and donor agency people. It was secluded at the National University of Lesotho at Roma for the purposes of concentration and lack of interruption. The Conference viewed the food system from several perspectives--agriculture, health, and community needs. Task force groups met to consider the new perspectives and then traditional ministry groups met to consider adaptations needed to accommodate the new concepts.

Conference consensus developed on three critical issues [15]. First, the dual problems of food aid dependence and reliance on miners' remittances to provide a large percentage of money for food imports were recognized. Should anything disturb these two external sources of food, the food system would experience severe imbalance. Second, food self-sufficiency should become a goal of the government of Lesotho. Third, activities to improve the food

19

system will contribute to general economic development in Lesotho in three specific ways. Better nutrition leads to improved health and more productive citizens. More efficient production, distribution, and consumption of food will be conducive to the optimum use of scarce resources. The creation of local food industries could provide local employment opportunities for the Basotho.

This consensus led to three basic objectives. First, the Food and Nutrition Council would be established to coordinate the nutrition work of the various agencies and thus foster inter-agency communication and integration in program planning and implementation. Second, a data center and research capability would be developed within Lesotho so that nutrition progress could be continually assessed. Third, a study of the entire food system would be undertaken to assess current operation and status, and possible improvements.

Figure 2.1 presents the organization of the Lesotho Nutrition Project, tracing the effort from the Conference to policy decisions. The nutritional status analysis was undertaken by the U.C.L.A. School of Public Health Nutrition Assessment Unit. It was directed by Dr. Fred Zerfas and Irwin Shorr. The study was designed to provide an objective measure of the food system by using anthropometry to evaluate the nutritional status of children under five. The operation of the food system was studied by means of four surveys: a consumer survey, farm survey, retailer survey, and industrial organization study. This aspect of the project was undertaken by the National University of Lesotho, under the guidance of Professor Charles Slater and Lee Dahringer of the University of Colorado. The methodology and results of this study is the subject of the balance of this chapter.

Methodology in Lesotho - The research mandate derived from the Conference led to a study of how the food system of Lesotho functions. The study provides a complete description from food source (both domestic and imported) to distribution to consumption.

The methods for this study are drawn in part from previous food system analysis. From 1965 through 1969, the Latin American Studies Center at Michigan State University conducted a series of studies in Puerto Rico, Brazil, Bolivia, and Colombia [19, 23, 21, 18]. From these studies, an initial group of interest areas were identified that corresponded to the needs and concerns of the Lesotho National Nutrition Conference. Survey instruments were designed and piloted on location to access issues and information needed. Each survey was translated from English

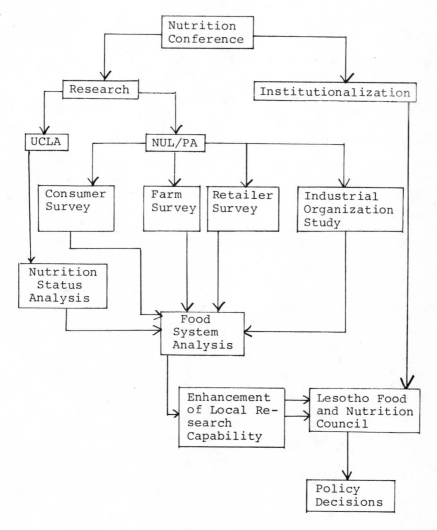

Figure 2.1   Lesotho Nutrition Project

Source: Strategies for Food System Enhancement in
          Lesotho through Developments in the Market
          Process Concept [4].

to Sesotho several times to minimize language difficulties. Before use in the field, each instrument sustained a minimum of five pilot revisions that helped to refine questions and areas of interest. In this manner, the points of concern as identified in the literature were combined with Conference considerations and conditions unique to Lesotho, and transformed into a series of survey instruments designed to gather the broad and comprehensive data required.

Because institutionalization was a stated goal of the Conference, the research was headquartered at the National University of Lesotho (NUL) at Roma. This location fostered the maximum participation of NUL people helped to develop the research capability within Lesotho. Planning Assistance team members, Charles Slater and Lee Dahringer, served as advisors to three faculty members and eleven students from NUL. The research capabilities which were tapped and developed now serve as a source of trained personnel able to undertake a systems analysis of virtually any problem and provide an objective data base to input into the decision process. This internal capability may provide employment, increased research technology, self-sufficiency in analysis, evaluation, monitoring of results, and ultimately, better policy decisions. The specific placement and utilization of this capability in Lesotho remains uncertain at the time of this writing, but the capability was enhanced by the food systems study.

Survey design and refinement, as outlined above, was accomplished during an intensive three week training program for the student interviewers. Training acquainted the team members with this particular project, as well as food and nutrition systems analysis in general. It provided continuity in survey design and application, and a thorough understanding of the methods and motivation of the project. The training session occurred in June 1976. Surveys were conducted from July through October, with surveys in the remote mountain areas completed by August. The substance of each survey will now be described. Practitioners interested in seeing the complete surveys are referred to Appendix A of Lee Dahringer's dissertation [4].

The Consumer and Household Survey sought to measure the consumer's interaction with and dependency on the food marketing system. It was directed by Lee Dahringer. The survey sought to determine the extent to which households utilized different sources of foods -- the marketplace, subsistence farming or

donated foods. Estimates of household expenditures
on food and drink, clothing and housing were recorded.
A series of questions on food received from clinics,
food-for-work and other donor agency projects attempted
to measure the impact of that sector. Food shopping
behavior and frequency questions were asked. The
frequency and purpose of travel to Maseru and other
nearby towns was investigated. Food purchases of the
household were compared to a standardized, pre-tested
shopping list. Attitude questions concerning consumer
satisfaction with the food system were discussed. In
short, the Consumer and Household Survey sought to
present a total picture of the food marketing system
as used and perceived by the consumer, including
farmers.

The Farm Survey concentrated on the conditions
and perceptions of small, subsistence farmers. It
was directed by Michael Sefali of the Economics
Department at NUL. Any households on the Consumer
Survey that reported deriving income from farming
were also interviewed by the Farm Survey. Questions
were asked concerning the amount of land held, type
of crops, livestock ownership, and the use and source
of farm inputs such as seeds, fertilizer, and power.
The amount and causes of crop damage were investigated. The extent and type of storage facilities
were discussed, as well as loss of product during
storage. Farmers were asked how they used their farm
products: how much and what types were kept for home
consumption and what was sold. Sources of farm credit,
capital, and information were examined. Inquiry was
made into problems facing the farmer and attitude
questions about farm practices were asked. In sum,
the Farm Survey measured the small farmer's degree
of market sophistication, his exposure to the market
channels, and the types and amounts of food available
to the farm family.

The Retailer Survey was directed by Phallang
Mokhesi, an instructor at the National University of
Lesotho. This survey investigated the attributes and
functioning of the market channel from the perspective
of the retailer. It asked questions concerning store
type, size, location, and products carried compared
to a predetermined model list. It sought information
about the purchase source of products, mode of transportation, wholesaler credit by product line, con-
signment selling, and storage space adequacy. The
number, relationship, and method of payment of store
employees were examined. Questions were asked about
capital sources and problems caused by capital shortage. The issues of customer services were probed,

including credit extension attitudes and practices.
Questions were asked concerning the potential market
for products made in Lesotho in an attempt to evaluate
the feasibility of import substitution. The prices
and costs of basic foodstuffs were examined. Finally,
attitude questions about perceived problems were asked
in order to invite the retailer to evaluate his own
situation and the overall performance of the market
system in Lesotho.

The Industrial Organization Study was conducted
by Clark Tibbits, lecturer at NUL. It concerned the
importation and wholesaling of food in Lesotho and
was the most politically sensitive issue covered by
the food system study. There was little prior research or comprehensive information on this subject
and thus the research itself was precedent setting.
Each interview of the major wholesalers and importers
was conducted by Tibbits himself in an effort to
provide continuity of research and help prevent
political pressure on this section and other aspects
of the research. The importers and wholesalers were
asked questions concerning business structure including size, number of outlets, and management practices.
Issues of capacity and competition were investigated.
Pricing policies were reviewed as were supply sources,
distribution practices, and product lines. Questions
were asked concerning the provision of customer services and perceived consumer values. In addition,
attitude questions were asked concerning the perceived obstacles to improved efficiency and the role
of importers/wholesalers in providing nutritionally
valuable foods. The data attained provided an analysis
of the food imports and wholesale food trade structure.
Interaction and evaluation is continuing to determine
whether suggestions for improved channel efficiency
will be generated from within the industry, and if
so, to assess the extent to which these suggestions
will improve the overall performance of the food
system.

The sampling procedure for all the surveys was
conducted under the direction of the Bureau of
Statistics of the government of Lesotho. This
coordination was essential to assure national representation and generalization. A systematic random
sample of 631 households was chosen for the Consumer
and Household Survey. Five hundred thirty-one (531)
of these households said that part of the household
income was derived from farming and these households
were included in the Farm Survey. Food retailers
that were found in the survey areas were included in
the Retailer Survey; they numbered 75. The Industrial

24

Organization Study concentrated on the seven largest
food importers as evidenced by national statistics.
These seven firms control 75 percent of the imported
food.

The 1976 Population Census was being tabulated
at the time of the study and preliminary results
were used in the sample design. The sampling procedure used a randomly chosen interval to select 19
enumeration areas, with an average of 33 interviews
in each. An enumeration area is a census survey area
and the number of interviews conducted in each area
varied with the population density. On a national
basis, the Consumer Survey and the Farm Survey allow
a 95 percent confidence level that the error will be
+ 4 percent when the survey response percentage is
50 percent.

The instruments described above provided a data
base for analysis of how the food system functions from
production through distribution to consumption. The
Kingdom of Lesotho National Nutrition Survey was
coordinated with the other surveys by sample design
and provided an objective measure of the performance
of the food system. The objective criteria investigated the nutritional well-being of the Basotho and
it was evaluated to assess the effectiveness of the
food system. The combined analysis can point to
systems failures, particularly in vulnerable groups
and regions, and help define policies and priorities.

The full details of the Kingdom of Lesotho
National Nutrition Survey will not be presented here:
interested readers are referred to the full U.C.L.A.
report [30]. The basic method of the study was to
use anthropometry to quantify malnutrition. The
survey investigated the nutritional status of children
under five and their mothers. For children, low
height or weight per age, or small arm circumference
were interpreted as indications of deficiencies in
protein and/or calories. Underweight was interpreted
as a sign of acute deficiency, usually recent in
character and frequently resulting from famine. Small
stature or height was interpreted as an indication
of a chronic shortage of caloric or protein intake.
Performance on these measures were compared to indices of "normal" children. The indices used here
were international reference median values for body
measures, as well as a reference group of children
in Maseru. The nutritional status of adults is more
difficult to define and measure. This study concentrated on clinical evidence of goiter and pellagra.

The National Nutrition Survey included questions
concerning the child's age, duration of breast feeding,

25

mother's age, number of live births of the mother,
number of children now alive, and clinic attendance
of the mother and child. It also reviewed household
information such as occupation of the head of household, relationship of household to child, number of
household workers in the R.S.A., household size, and
possession of livestock. In addition, the sources of
milk and food were investigated: for example, did
household members receive food from direct farm
consumption, clinic, school, or market.

The conclusions of the National Nutrition Survey
can be outlined briefly. One in five children was
found to be chronically undernourished and below
growth potential. Acute protein-calorie malnutrition
was found in 3 percent of the children. Children aged
two to five months showed the least prevalence of
undernutrition which probably can be attributed to the
protective influence of breast-feeding. For children
two to five years old, 25 percent were anemic, and
two percent showed signs of severe anemia. Nutritional
status was found to be more adequate in urban areas,
but throughout Lesotho there was a high number of
children in borderline or high-risk groups.

For the mothers surveyed, the evidence is less
conclusive. Five percent showed evidence of under-
nourishment and ten percent were probably undernourished during childhood. Ten percent of the mothers
were characterized by low stature, and three percent
had low arm circumference. However, 21 percent overall showed signs of obesity, concentrated in the urban
areas. In addition, four percent of the mothers had
clinical signs of goiter, but few showed any evidence
of pellagra. (The pellagra finding was probably
influenced by the fact that the survey was conducted
in the spring when green vegetables are available in
homestead gardens and by collection of wild vegetation.)

In short, the Kingdom of Lesotho National Nutrition Survey indicates that the food system of Lesotho
is not providing adequate nutrition to all citizens.
Although the nutritional status does not seem to be
as poor as one might expect, there are many people
in borderline high risk groups. It can be inferred
that the nutrition of these vulnerable groups will be
adversely affected by any downward change in food
supply.

Description of the Food System of Lesotho - The
channel mapping methodology as described above provides a description of the food system of Lesotho.
This section will present the highlights of that
description: the full details are available in the
report to the Lesotho Food and Nutrition Council [20].

First a diagram of the food system will be given. Its elements will be discussed, starting with the components of food supply and then outlining aspects of food demand. This description will be followed by some general conclusions about current food system performance and then a brief discussion of contingent problems. Finally, some priorities for food system improvement will be suggested.

Figure 2.2 presents a paradigm of the food system of Lesotho, with 1976 national value estimates. The diagram begins with the sources of demand for food and then combines these for total effective demand. This demand is met by various sources in the food system and how it is met determines the distribution of food as well as the nutritional performance of the food system. Forty-five percent of the food consumed in Lesotho comes from subsistence agriculture. (The value of R26 million is an imputed value of farm product and is not actually part of the cash economy.) Thirty-one percent of the food is commercially imported. Thirteen percent is domestically produced and marketed. Fully eleven percent of Lesotho's food is donated by other nations.

Figure 2.2 highlights three critical problems which face the food system of Lesotho. First, Lesotho imports almost one-third of its food. This dependence indicates lack of a sufficient production system and necessitates an outflow of funds that contributes to the need for migrant labor and food donations from other nations. Second, Lesotho annually receives donated foods valued at U.S. $7 million. These foods are a necessary component of the food system; they fill a critical gap in food supply and they are fairly well distributed. However, they are drawing some people away from food production in Lesotho and are depressing food prices for locally produced food. In addition, the question of continuity of this supply re-inforces Lesotho's dependence on external sources. Third, the diagram shows that current supply just barely meets current demand. Many elements of the population experience significant risk of nutritional deficiency and there is no leeway in the system for unequal distribution. When these issues are compounded by the demands of a growing population, the food system seems dangerously strained.

The food supply in Lesotho can be described by survey results concerning direct farm consumption, marketed farm surplus, imported foods, and donated foods. Eighty-four percent of the households in Lesotho farm, with an average land holding of 3.5 acres. Seventy-two percent own livestock, 70 percent

27

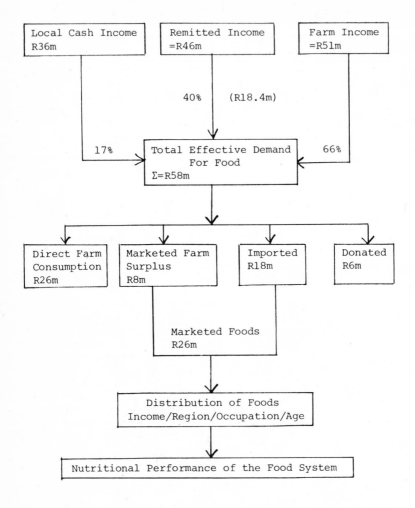

Figure 2.2 Paradigm of the Food System (With 1976 National
Value Estimates)

Note: Percentages indicate proportions of income utilized
for food.

Source: An Exploratory Study of the Food System of Lesotho:
A Report to the Lesotho Food and Nutrition
Council [20].

28

have homestead gardens, and 60 percent own fruit
trees. Eighty percent of the farms raise maize and
sorghum, wheat and beans are other important crops.
Fifty percent of the households collect wild vegetables to supplement their diet.

Lesotho farms can be characterized by their low
use of farm inputs, with many farmers attributing
this trend to a lack of farm capital. Only 20 percent of the farms use chemical fertilizer, with
another 11 percent using manure to fertilize. Pesticides are used on only four percent of the farms.
Eighty-eight percent of the farms use oxen as the
source of power for plowing and 94 percent of the
harvesting is done by hand. Fifty-nine percent of
the farmers report that they practice crop rotation.
Forty-three percent of the farms lose part of their
output due to poor storage facilities; it is estimated
that approximately 16 percent of expected output is
lost because of this problem. Seventy-five percent
of the farmers use their own seed as stock for the
next planting cycle. Although many recognize that
this practice may re-inforce the cycle of low productivity, high prices are usually cited as the major
deterrent to purchasing new seeds.

Approximately 70 percent of all farm product is
used for direct farm consumption by the farming household. The other 30 percent is sold: 18 percent
of it is exported and 82 percent is marketed domestically. In short, Lesotho households are significantly dependent upon direct farm consumption. Their
farms are characterized by low technology and labor
intensive practices.

Approximately 60 percent of all Lesotho farmers
sell some of their farm output to the commercial
marketing channels. However, this marketed output
accounts for only 13 percent of the total food supply.
Some of the marketed output is exported and then imported again after processing in the R.S.A. The
exact amount and value of domestically marketed foods
is difficult to determine because there are many informal barter arrangements and frequently farm measurement practices are not standardized. However,
commercial channels are the most commonly used outlets for marketed surplus. The wholesale and retail
channels buy and sell local products as well as deal
in imports and exports. Their operation will be
discussed under imported foods.

Marketed imports provide 30 percent of the food
consumed, and when this is combined with marketed
farm surplus, fully 45 percent of Lesotho's food
travels through commercial market channels.

Wholesalers and retailers handle most of this food.

There are twenty-one food wholesalers in Lesotho, but six of them control 75% of the wholesale food trade. These six carry similar product lines. Primarily they stock packaged goods with long shelf life. They seldom have fresh meat or vegetables and only powdered or canned milk is stocked. Oranges are the only fruit that is consistently available. Almost all imports and exports travel through the Republic of South Africa and many of the wholesalers are owned by R.S.A. firms. In general, wholesalers are not aware of nutrition as an issue, but they did express interest in their potential role for improving the performance of the food system.

Lesotho has almost three thousand food retailers. These include general dealers, cafes, grocers, butchers, bakers, and green grocers. They are concentrated in the urban areas and the urban stores have slightly lower prices and greater selection. The retailers interviewed indicated that family savings is the source of capital for their stores and therefore capital is limited. Only 15 percent of the retailers reported that they bought on credit, but 75 percent sold on credit. Damage in transit, credit to customers, and prices were cited as the major problems that retailers faced. The retailers viewed purchasing power as a bottleneck in the nutrition system since 64 percent said that a lack of funds prevented customers from buying necessities. Ninety-eight percent of the retailers said that they would stock items made in Lesotho if price and quality were comparable to imported items.

In addition to direct farm consumption, marketed farm surplus, and food imports, donated foods are a major source of nutrients in Lesotho. Donated foods are essential to the Basotho diet and supply approximately ten percent of all foods consumed. Donated foods are non-trade imports, with cereals and cereal products comprising more than half of what is received. The major distributors of donated foods in Lesotho are the Catholic Relief Service and the World Food Programme. The major outlets of this food to the consumer are pre-school clinic programs, school lunch programs, and food for work projects. Donated foods are reaching some of the nutritionally vulnerable groups in Lesotho. The targeting of the foods could be improved, but it is not wasteful or inefficient. Donated foods fill a critical gap and without them, the food system would deliver significantly inadequate nutrition to many households. However, this extreme dependence is a continuing source of national insecurity for the Basotho.

The demand for food in Lesotho can be described by discussing survey results concerning sources of household income and how it is spent. The basic diet for the rural population (94 percent of all the Basotho) is very limited in variety. It consists primarily of maize porridge as the main dish with a protein or vegetable relish. How much each household and each individual consumes is uncertain and should be investigated by a food consumption survey.

The average household annually spends close to R200 on food. This is 50 percent of the family's cash income and buys approximately 60 percent of the calories consumed. Forty percent of the households shop for food on a daily basis and 80 percent walk to and from the store. In general, consumers are dissatisfied with the commercial food channels and seem distrustful of pricing and service policies.

There are three basic sources of food demand: local cash income, remitted cash, and farm income (both in cash and kind). The food system study asked for self-reports on these sources, but in many instances these reports are inconsistent with other sources of information. This inconsistency means that it is more difficult to assess the demand for food than the supply, and it also underscores the need for more research into this area.

The issue of remitted cash income from individuals employed in the R.S.A. is an area of significant discrepancy. The self-report measure indicates that an average of R140 is remitted annually to households in Lesotho. However, the mining company estimates are much higher. Partial explanation for this difference may be that money is sent home for special expenditures and therefore it may be overlooked in the self-report measures that are primarily concerned with subsistence. In addition, much of the money value that is remitted is brought to Lesotho in the form of goods that are imported by individuals returning from the R.S.A. Thus, it is difficult to ascertain which estimate for remittances is the most accurate and this makes it difficult to determine amounts of income available for food purchases.

Farm income is also difficult to measure precisely. Again there is the problem that self-report measures are frequently over-stated or under-stated deliberately, or through inaccurate appraisal of the situation. In addition, production estimates are hampered by the lack of standardization and market uncertainties. Therefore, farm income is also uncertain.

Local cash income is more certain because it is monitored by government agencies. However, this source represents only a small percentage of the total food demand and primarily affects only urban households.

Within the limitation of these uncertain sources, a model family was derived with estimates of effective demand. Then an analysis of the required food intake for the family was made. These two models were integrated to analyze the question of whether income can provide the needed calories. This analysis shows that the average Basotho family is just at the borderline: the available income is barely adequate to provide the minimum calories required. Thirty percent of Basotho families are below the model family in income and thus they are experiencing shortfalls in income that put them in high risk of nutritional deficiency. The most vulnerable are non-miner households, older families, and people without land, and there is a regional uniformity in the distribution. These results are reasonably consistent with the National Nutrition Survey: there is some nutritional inadequacy currently and many households and individuals are in high risk situations.

The general conclusion of the food system study is that even with high levels of donated foods, the food system of Lesotho is delivering only barely adequate nutrition. Therefore the question becomes one of future needs and contingencies. Will the food system be able to meet the nutritional needs of Lesotho's future considering the variables of population growth, erosion and possible curtailment of Basotho employment in the R.S.A.?

The 1976 census reported Lesotho's population to be 1,210,906. With the projected 2.3 percent annual growth, the population will increase by 400,000 in a decade. This increased population will inevitably cause a severe strain on the food system. The demand for food will increase, but some of it will probably not be economically effective demand and therefore the need for donated foods will increase. In addition, increased population will amplify the stress on the market channel infrastructure. Perhaps the most detrimental effect of increased population is that population growth tends to concentrate among the rural poor, a trend which distorts the distribution of food. Thus the vulnerable groups will find their condition worsening.

This study did not investigate the problem of erosion except by informal observations and the report by 65 percent of the farmers that erosion is a

constraint on the production of their farms. It seems
an inescapable fact that erosion is a serious and
growing problem in Lesotho. Estimates are that up to
one percent of the land erodes each year. The land
is strained by over-use: some acres are cultivated
that should not be and the soil quality is deteriorating. Unless these trends are offset by conservation and good land use policy and practice, the
problem can only get worse.

If the employment of Basotho labor in the Republic
of South Africa is curtailed, the return of the miners
will have two direct impacts on the food system of
Lesotho. The cash remittances will cease, and with
the miners home, the daily direct demand for food
will increase. Since households depend on cash for
45 percent of their food intake, if the remittances
stop and cash income falls, nutritional adequacy will
be adversely affected. The return of the miners might
increase agricultural production since more male labor
would be available during the land preparation phases
of farming. However, this increase in production
would not be nearly enough to offset the increased
demand for food. In addition, many miners do not own
land and do not want to return to being farmers. This
will probably lead to increased levels of urban un-
employment and greater numbers of urban poor. These
trends can only cause more strain on the food system.
Finally if the miners return home permanently, population growth rates will increase and exacerbate the
problems already delineated.

It can be concluded that the future will be a
stiff challenge for the food system of Lesotho. The
system is faltering now and the problems threaten
to grow much worse. There is an immediate and drastic
need for effective programs to combat these trends.

Strategies for Enhancing the Performance of
the Food System - By its very nature, this kind of
analysis suggests points of intervention and possible
strategies for improvement. The study measures the
attitudes of channel participants and consumers, and
asks for perceived problems and causes. It emphasizes
areas where change will be most effective: since 58
percent of the food consumed comes from direct farm
consumption and domestically marketed surplus, and
another 31 percent comes through the market channels
as imports, then programs to enhance the subsistence
sector and the marketing system will probably achieve
the most beneficial results. By following these
clues, a series of enhancement strategies were derived.

The methodology described in this chapter views the provision of adequate nutrition as an objective function of the society. It is an elemental need and the structures of the community are considered to be responsible for providing the opportunity for meeting the need. Therefore, improvements may involve the distribution of income, food production and distribution systems, and import/export policy as well as the more traditional approaches of consumer nutrition education, nutrition related health projects, and food supplements to vulnerable groups. By viewing the food system as a closed system from production through distribution to consumption, a more comprehensive and integrated program of improvement can be developed.

Before presenting specific enhancement strategies, food system issues should be discussed in relation to development planning. Because the food system is critical to all members of all societies, it exhibits a wide range of involvement and affects many vital functions and activities. Therefore it is interconnected with many of the issues of economic development.

Recently other nations in development have started to emphasize programs to assist small farmers, rather than schemes to assist large scale agricultural producers [8, 17]. This trend seems consistent with the facts in Lesotho since the small farmer is the source of most of the food, and small scale retailers are a primary source of marketed foods.

Figures 2.3 and 2.4 present contrasting paradigms for technology transfer. Comparison of these two diagrams indicates that the transfer of inappropriate technology has far-reaching negative consequences for the entire social fabric of the society. It weakens the family, causes an increase in the number of urban poor, and fosters political instability. Conversely, the transfer of appropriate technology has more beneficial, stabilizing and egalitarian results. It may be less easily developed and applied, but it produces solid, effective change. The food system of Lesotho needs a balanced effort with emphasis on traditional direct farm and village production and consumption, as well as support for integrated large scale programs.

The food system study recommended four categories of strategies for improving nutrition in Lesotho: enhancing direct farm consumption, increasing domestic production of commercial foods, improving consumer performance, and the institutionalization of nutrition programs. Full discussion of

34

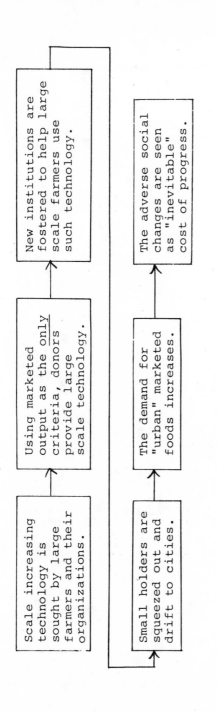

Figure 2.3 Paradigm of Transfer of Inappropriate Technology

Source: An Exploration Study of the Food System of Lesotho: A Report to the Lesotho Food and Nutrition Council [20].

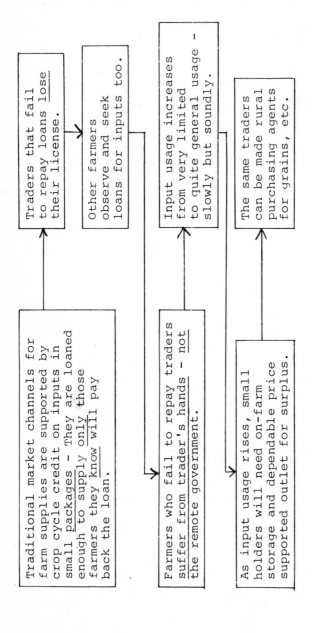

Figure 2.4 Paradigm of Transfer of Appropriate Technology

Source: An Exploratory Study of the Food System of Lesotho: A Report to
the Lesotho Food and Nutrition Council [20].

36

these strategies is presented in the report to the
Lesotho Food and Nutrition Council [20]. This section
will present a summary discussion.

Since direct farm consumption provides 45 percent of the food consumed in Lesotho, improving the
performance of subsistence farmers will undoubtedly
improve general nutrition levels. Farmers recognize
that a lack of farm inputs is a constraint on farm
production. Therefore availability of farm inputs
including seed, fertilizer and pesticides should be
improved. If these inputs were available in packages
that are manageable in size at local commercial outputs where credit might be provided, then use would
probably increase. A second improvement that would
increase farm production would be to provide better
methods of storage to diminish crop loss. Possible
methods of improved storage include better drying
techniques, more adequate storage containers, and the
use of pesticides after harvest. A series of feasibility studies is needed to determine the appropriate
scale of possible methods and to insure storage control by owners. Another needed policy is price
support for locally produced food. The price must be
linked to prices of farm commodities in the Republic
of South Africa so that Basotho farmers will be assured
of a market for their produce. Without this policy,
Basotho farmers endure much risk in producing farm
products and frequently suffer a loss in the marketplace. The finaly policy recommended specifically
for direct farm production is a silage program to
assure that oxen are fit for plowing in the spring.
It was discovered that the food cycle for oxen often
leaves them too weak to plow in the spring when their
performance is most critical to the farm cycle. If
silage programs were instituted so that fodder could
be stored through the winter and fed to the oxen in
the early spring, this situation could be ameliorated.

Since self-sufficiency in food is one of the
stated goals of the Lesotho National Nutrition Conference, and the food system study indicates that
only a small percentage of the commercial food source
is domestically supplied, a second group of strategies
were recommended to increase the supply of locally
produced food. First, a series of land improvement
programs should be undertaken to increase the tillable
acreage available and reduce erosion. Recommended
programs include contour plowing, crop rotation, vine
planting to control dongas, perenniel plantings of
croppable vines, bushes and trees, and the more
capital intensive measures of irrigation and
terracing. These programs are an immediate necessity

37

in order to restore the land as a resource. A second
recommendation is to encourage the local processing of
foods. Small local mills for maize could be established.
This would keep food processing jobs in Lesotho, help
keep prices for processed foods lower, and help maintain
the nutrient value of the food consumed. Another
recommendation for enhancing local production of food
involves contingency projects in case employment in
the R.S.A. is curtailed. Possible projects include
road construction and maintenance, land development
such as terracing and flood control measures, and
possibly cropping in the high valleys. This kind of
contingency planning will help to avert any major
nutritional discontinuities and will also help to
develop national self-reliance.

In the final analysis, the performance of the
food system can only be evaluated by assessing the
nutritional status of individuals. Therefore a set
of comprehensive programs to improve the food system
must include a series of strategies directed toward
the behavior and status of the consumer. Two of these
recommendations are designed to facilitate the consumers' interaction with the commercial food system.
Training clinics for wholesalers and retailers should
be held periodically to help make the commercial
channel system more efficient and lower cost. Methods
to serve the consumer better should be derived from
the traders' participation in these sessions as well
as from government guidelines. It was also recommended
that food standards legislation should be enacted to
control and improve imports and sales. These standards should improve the quality of food that is
delivered to the consumer and also build his confidence in the commercial food system. Another
recommendation is aimed directly at the consumer.
It was suggested that a consumer education program on
nutrition should be undertaken by the commercial
channels and Extension services. Also, mobile health
clinics should be organized with Extension skills in
all aspects of nutrition. It was recommended that
existing programs for nutritionally vulnerable groups
should be thoroughly evaluated and re-directed where
necessary. Finally, the food system study recommended
that family planning assistance should be made available to all households in Lesotho, particularly those
which are in nutritional high risk groups.

In order to monitor and coordinate all nutrition
policy in Lesotho, it was recommended that one central
government agency should take the responsibility for
nutrition policy evaluation and planning. This agency
should have decision-making authority and should also

have direct access to the highest officials in
Lesotho's government. At the time of this writing,
this recommendation had been implemented and the
Lesotho Food and Nutrition Council has assumed its
role as program designer and coordinator. In order to
provide the Council with a sound data base for policy
decisions, the capability for policy and monitoring
research has been established at the National University of Lesotho.

Conclusions - The food system study of Lesotho
demonstrates that the channel mapping technique
described is a relatively quick and inexpensive
analysis that provides an improved data base, comprehensive suggestions for system revision, greater
institutionalization, and improved decision-making.
In Lesotho, the food system was studied from production to distribution to consumption, with complete
channel mappings at each level. In addition, the
National Nutrition Survey investigated individual
nutritional status as an objective measure of the
performance of the system. The channel mapping
procedure provided a clear and complete description
of one of the most critical sectors of the society.

Generalization to Other Life Support Systems and
Other Nations

The Lesotho research is presented only as a
prototype illustration of the quality and quantity
of data which results from a channel mapping exercise.
The procedure itself, as described earlier in this
chapter is neutral with regard to life support systems
analysis. That is, the procedures and techniques
described in detail here are applicable to other life
support systems research in other nations. For
example, channel mappings can be done and objective
criteria of performance can be evaluated for housing,
energy, clothing, health, safety, and education. The
vertical integration of a series of mappings will
provide an overview of the entire society and from
this holistic description, a closed system analysis
can be derived.

The issues for each life support sector will
differ, but the methods of research can be similar.
Surveys of channel participants will give the most
comprehensive view of their performance and perspectives.
Generalizations from the survey data can give a
comprehensive view of the system as well as suggestions for improvement. In some sectors, the objective
criteria may be difficult to determine, but consideration of societal expectations and minimum requirements

will usually provide insight into performance
standards.

Each community should work to understand the
functions and performance of the life support systems.
Thorough investigation will reveal the minimum requirements for political stability and effective
social change. Improving the policy formation process
requires a better information base about micro institutions and the links between the micro and macro
goals of the community. More accurate information
can lead to more effective policy formation and contingency planning and thus ease transition in Southern
Africa.

The information that is derived from the technique
described in this chapter provides a complete system
analysis and can thus be used without further development. However, this kind of information can also be
utilized in a more formal model of trade-off assessment to improve public decision-making. Chapter III
describes an input/output simulation model that can
use this descriptive information to evaluate alternative policies.

III. Simulation Model of the Transition to Majority Rule in Rhodesia

   Significant socio-economic changes, whether
gradual or abrupt, require a careful assessment of
the trade-offs associated with change and with policy
responses to that change. Because such changes affect
a wide range of interactive variables, and have general welfare consequences, the assessment of associated
trade-offs is critical. Without thorough evaluation
of change, policy decisions will be inadequate.
Changes can be internally or externally induced, but
in either case the character and dimension of the
impact of the initial shock to the system need to be
described and evaluated. In turn, the secondary
effects of the perturbations can be described and
measured. Descriptive research like the Lesotho food
system study can provide a comprehensive description
of the existing system. However, illumination of
major changes in the system cannot be immediately
derived from the initial descriptive research but
frequently must be investigated by additional systems
research. This can be inefficient in terms of time
and money. In terms of choosing between alternative
policy mixes, it can only be a trial and error method.
Therefore, a technique is needed to build on this
descriptive research and provide trade-off assessment for different policies.
   Simulation modeling is a promising method for
assessing trade-offs. But simulation has only become
practical with the improvement in several research
techniques. Before social science provided reliable
household budget surveys and input/output descriptions
of economic processes, simulations were often inaccurate. Furthermore, before large scale computers,
simulations were unmanageably large mathematical
problems. Thus it is only in the last two decades
that the technology has emerged for these approaches

to policy review and decision. Work on the elements of input/output simulations has increased rapidly. One development has been the emergence of the DIOSIM concept.

The rudimentary elements of the DIOSIM (Dynamic Input/Output Simulation) concept evolved from partial equilibrium models of the impact of the modernization of the food systems of Puerto Rico and the Recife area of Brazil [19, 23]. From this beginning, the DIOSIM system of equations was developed by Charles Slater and Geoffrey Walsham in Kenya during 1973 and 1974. The original model of the Kenyan economy was used to assess the 1974-78 Development Plan [26, 25, 24]. It provided useful insights into the planning process and helped assess the trade-offs associated with alternative strategies. Sin-e that original application in Kenya, DIOSIM has had three major policy applications: (1) a model of the Rhodesian economy to assess the transition to majority rule [25], (2) a model of the United States economy for validation and sensitivity testing of simulation models [16], and (3) a model of the state of Colorado to evaluate the impact of the 1976-77 drought [22].

This chapter will first present a description of the DIOSIM framework and then describe the Rhodesian application of the model. Full listings of the model equations, code, and data sources are included in Appendix I.

Essential Features of DIOSIM

The rapidly developing problems associated with transition to majority rule in Rhodesia can affect future development. Therefore, there is a need to foster flexibility in planning response to change. The problem is that complex changes are likely to occur from multiple causal factors, and therefore, in most cases, the impact of the changes is not intuitively obvious. Since the casual factors cannot be conveniently disaggregated and considered one at a time, analysis is complex. A systems model that simulates the Rhodesian economy is one way to consider the interactive responses to multiple changes. Such a model has been constructed and applied to the present set of expected changes. It is computerized and ready to be applied in the future if events conspire to make current estimates of change obsolete.

The model of Rhodesia began with a sensitivity assessment of the Kenyan model's system of equations to assess whether the model would remain stable when some of the major parameter estimates of Rhodesia

42

were used instead of Kenyan data. The model seemed
stable. The model structure was then adapted to the
task of assessing the significant changes that were
likely to be associated with transition in Rhodesia.
    Figure 3.1 presents the basic relationships of
DIOSIM. The model contains five major areas of
activity: a consolidated input/output table, a sales
component, a dissaggregated household sector, a capital
formation process, and a government sector. The in-
put/output sector contains ten production centers:

1. a traditional subsistence rural economic
   sector,

2. a modern agricultural sector,

3. a manufacturing sector,

4. a building and construction sector,

5. a utility sector,

6. a commercial sector,

7. a transportation sector,

8. a services sector,

9. a mining sector,

10. a government sector.

These ten production sectors engage in inter-industry
transfers as well as turning out end use products and
services. The input/output (I/O) is initially set at
the base year, chosen as 1971 in Rhodesia. The I/O
operates in the usual manner of Leontief models for
most of its operations, calling for imports, labor
and inter-industry transfers to generate final demand
output and residual income to sector and for reinvestment or distribution as profits. The model is
unusual in that both wages and profits are disaggregated into nine income class recipients, so that the
distribution of income is an output of the model.
    The model is also unusual in that the final de-
manded output of the ten sectors is funnelled through
the five sectors from which consumers acquire goods
and services. The model has, in effect, a market
channel aggregation of output that resembles the real
world more closely than most traditional I/O models.
An important advantage of this type of channelling of
output through market channels is that the more realistic conduits for goods and services are fewer.
With only three commercial channels (commerce, services, utilities) and two non-commercial channels

Figure 3.1   SCHEMATIC DIAGRAM OF DIOSIM
(Arrows indicate direction of money flows.)

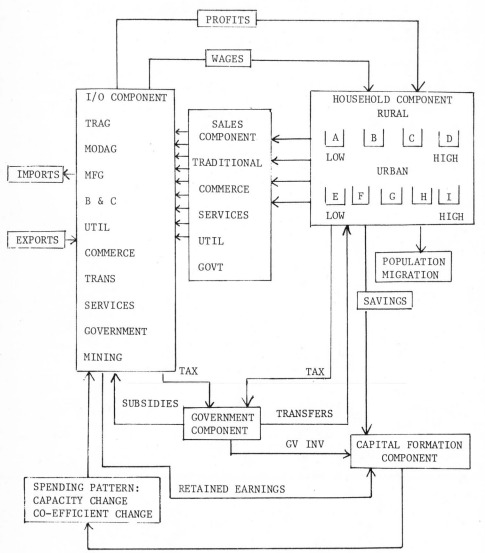

(traditional and government) that are each price inelastic, the effects of cross elasticities of demand with respect to price are to some extent constrained. Thus price elasticity effects can be treated as exogenous rather than endogenous processes. A more highly disaggregated input/output model would no doubt require a different and more complex treatment of price effects.

The household sector contains four rural household income classes, a transitional group of low income urban people, and four urban household income classes with wage and profit incomes above a subsistence level. The real incomes of each of the nine classes remain constant over time, but the money income rises with inflation. The number of people in each class is affected by the distribution of income from transfers as well as wages and profits. Thus the distribution of income, once transfer policy is set, is endogenously derived by the model.

Capital formation is generated from savings of households, retained earnings and depreciation, government investment and foreign capital investment. Investment in any given sector has a spending pattern. This allows the investment to be allocated to three recipients: the sector itself, the services sector, and the building and construction sector. Investment will demand construction, increase the capacity of the sector, and also alter the technical co-efficients of the sector to which it is applied. Presently, these spending patterns are constant over time, but differ among sectors.

Government behaves as both a sector of the input output table and a center of model activity. As an input output sector, government behaves in much the same way as the other sector: it employs workers and engages in inter-industry transfers. It is necessary in the I/O to balance the table. However, the more comprehensive concept of government is embodied in the government activity center of DIOSIM. The government component collects taxes, borrows money, and spends money on debt service, capital formation, subsidies, and consumption. It also provides funds for transfers directly to households in various income classes.

Figure 3.2 presents a simplified flow chart of the model sequence. (A complete flow chart is included in Appendix I.) After the initial parameterization and balancing, the technical coefficients of change are derived by using second year data and difference equations to calculate the difference rates which will be used throughout the simulation. Next, the first standard year of model output is

45

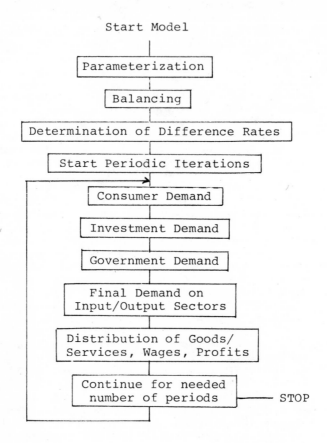

Figure 3.2   Sequence of Model Operation

started. Since the model is demand driven, the calculations for each year begin with three sources of
demand: consumer demand, government demand, and investment demand. Total consumer demand on the productive sectors is determined by the income distribution of the prior period and consumption propensi-
ties. Also consumer taxes, savings, and direct imports are calculated. Government income is calculated
as the sum of taxes, duties, and loans, but annual
government expenditure is an exogenous policy variable.
Thus government consumption and investment demand is
read into the model and a government deficit figure
is calculated as the difference between the internal
income figure and the imposed expenditure figure.
Investment demand is calculated as the sum of consumer savings, business savings, government capital
expenditure, and private capital imports. Capital
investment generates increased demand on the construction and services sectors, increases the capacity
of the sector, and alters the sector's technical coefficients. Export and stock change figures are read
into the model and final demand is calculated as the
sum of consumer demand, government demand, investment
demand, exports, and stock changes.

Final demand is then applied to the productive
sectors. Standard input/output analysis is used to
generate the gross output required from the productive
sectors. If demand exceeds the capacity constraint
for any sector, the remaining demand is met by imports.

Given the final output of the productive sectors
and the levels of inflation, calculations are made for
wages and profits to consumers, total business taxes,
reinvestment into sectors, and intermediate imports.
Payments are distributed to income classes based on
population growth and migration rates, together with
endogenous data on consumer income and inflation
levels. From this calculation, the total population
is redistributed among income classes. The number
from each income class that is engaged in wage employment in each sector is also calculated. This final
distribution of payments determines the consumer demand, government demand, and investment demand for
the next year, and the model is ready to go through
the operational sequence again.

Data Requirements (DIOSIM)

One of the unique features of the DIOSIM class
of models is that the data requirements are relatively
simple and usually available in the published statistics of the economic region to be modelled. This

feature is a distinct advantage over the complex data
requirement of most simulation models and it generally
allows the DIOSIM framework to be applied to an area
with comparative speed. The Rhodesian model was made
operational in two months using published data,
supplemented by insights from KENSIM.

DIOSIM's data is comprised of three decks.
Deck I contains the data for the base year. The base
year can be any comparatively stable year for which
input/output analysis, national income accounts, and
consumer survey data are available. It is usually
set several years before the time when policy analysis
will be made so that there are years available for
historic tracking and model calibration.

Deck II contains the data for the next historic
year and provides the information used in deriving
the difference equations of the model.

Deck III is a series of periodic inputs which
are compiled for each year for which the model is run.
This deck provides historic data in the years for which
it is available. In later years, for which historic
data does not exist, periodic data is estimated by
regression techniques, set at a low but steady growth
rate, entered at a stable inflation rate, or set as
policy variables. The user has access to the data
inputs of Deck III and by changing them from the base
level, different scenarios are modelled and policy
runs are made.

The following list of variables must be generated
by the model user on an annual basis. These are the
model inputs that can be used to simulate scenarios
and policy options:

    -- government investment by sector,
    -- government debt and debt service,
    -- government consumption, capital formation,
       and subsidies,
    -- private foreign investment,
    -- exports and stock changes by sector,
    -- capital capacity ratios (the proportions
       of units of capital needed to generate
       units of output),
    -- technical coefficient changes to inputs,
       imports, wages, rents, interest, deprecia-
       tion and taxes by sector,
    -- price changes of imports, wages, rents,
       depreciation, interest, and taxes,
    -- weather factor,
    -- population growth and urbanization rates,
    -- emigration rates,
    -- agricultural demand shift factor.

48

It should be emphasized here that DIOSIM is not
a forecasting model. It is parameterized to identify
a base level of the economy. It is projected into
the future at a low but stable growth rate that does
not reflect a forecast. Rather, a base is generated
as a benchmark to which changes and alternate strategies can be compared. This distinction is critical
in understanding the results of the model. All
scenarios must be compared to the base in order to
provide meaningful analysis.

Output from DIOSIM

The simulation model reports four kinds of information: "base year data echo check," transformation coefficients, accounting balance check, and
annual simulation reports. The character of this
information is described below.

Base Year Data Echo Check - Input data for the
base year period is reported as it is interpreted by
the model. Headings describe data types (for
example, input/output, imports) and the data is presented by sector or income class. The scale of the
data is reported in scientific notation.

Balance Checks - Three accounting balance checks
are made and reported:

(1) Household income is calculated by income
class by three methods. All three should derive the
same figures for each income class. The calculations
are, household income equals:

> (a) (income per household) x (number of
>   households per class)
>
> (b) the sum of wages, rents, and trans-
>   fers by income class
>
> (c) the sum of taxes, savings, and
>   consumption by income class.

(2) Household consumption is calculated from
the consumption matrix where traditional agriculture,
utilities, commerce, services, and government are
considered to be the channels for all consumption.
Consumption for the above sectors should equal the
money value of the conversion matrix for the above
sectors. Note that the conversion matrix distributes
direct demand from the five distribution sectors to
demand on all ten input/output sectors.

(3) Consumption of the ten sectors is calculated
as the sum of inputs, imports, wages, rents, depreciation, interest, indirect taxes, intermediate imports,
less subsidies, stock changes, exports, and investment.

The above consumption by sector is contrasted with
consumption as defined by the conversion matrix.

Coefficient Matrices and Vectors - Matrices
representing I/O, private wages, and rents in the
base period are converted into coefficient matrices
as a proportion of gross output by sector. Vectors
representing imports, depreciation, interest, and
indirect taxes are calculated as a proportion of
gross output per sector. Sector capacities are calculated as a function of capacity utilization and
gross output per sector. The above coefficients are
reported as a part of the base period output.

Annual Output - The first two years of model
output do not follow the standard format for the
other years. After presenting the balance checks
and diagnostics described above, some derived data
for the second year is reported. For the remainder
of the modelled years, the elements of output for
each year are the same.

Each year begins with a report of direct consumption demand on the four marketing sectors, traditional agriculture, utilities, commerce and services. Then consumer demand on the ten processing
sectors is reported, followed by constrained demand
on the ten sectors. Next consumer taxes, consumer
savings, and direct consumption imports are reported.
Then the model enumerates a series of figures on
government: government income, expenditure, deficit,
and consumption demand on the government sector.
Next capital formation by sector and the construction
effect of capital investment are reported. Then the
derived figure for final demand is reported together
with figures for provisional capacity value for each
sector.

After these reports on the various elements of
demand as generated by the model, a series of
diagnostics is printed. These report the changes
in technical coefficients; this information is useful
to the technical analysts but does not provide insight into the results of scenarios or policy.

Next the model outputs a series of information
about annual production. First provisional gross
output of each sector is reported, this is the unconstrained production of each sector in response to
demand. Next the final output of each sector is
reported. Here the capacity constraints have been
accounted for, and the difference between demand and
final output is reported to be imported.

The prices of outputs are calculated as a result
of price changes in imports, wages, rents, depreciation, interest, and taxes. These price changes are

50

exogenously assigned, but they are reported by the model for easy reference just before the output price changes are reported. The output price changes are followed by report of the new capacity value.

Inflation factors are then derived and reported for each income class. Assuming the same consumption patterns, the inflation factors are used to derive new household income levels in current dollars. These new levels are reported by the model. Based on the new price of output, and on wages, rents, and transfers paid to income classes by government and the processing sectors, the number of households in each income class is derived. The numbers in each class are reported for four rural and five urban classes. The number in income classes is reported twice: first, as the unconstrained result of the income distribution algorithm, and then as the result of policy constraining migration into urban areas.

The final annual output of the model is the matrix of wage employment. The number of individuals in each income class that are employed by each productive sector is reported. In addition, the total number of wage employed per class is presented.

The economic growth rates for individual sectors and the overall economy are reported each year in the section of output that reports on annual production. The overall growth rate of the economy for the model period is the final piece of information at the end of the last year of output.

The Rhodesian Simulation: Transition and Development

As a part of the United States Agency for International Development Southern African Task Force activities of November 1976 through February 1977, a DIOSIM model of the Rhodesian economy was developed. It was computerized and applied to sixteen broad changes in three simulated cases. The structure of the model was discussed in the preceding section, and this section describes the Rhodesian application.

The possible patterns of transition to majority rule in Rhodesia range from a very orderly and gradual process to a violent and extended civil war. This simulated analysis considers only an essentially non-violent transition in which private and government market exchange remain the dominant forms of production and distribution. The possibility of this type of transition is becoming increasingly dubious, but this simulation analysis was undertaken in 1976 when civil war did not seem inevitable.

Rhodesia in transition is confronted by two sets
of problems: transitional problems and development
problems. This distinction fosters analysis even
though the timing and effects of the two sets merge.
The transitional problems can be divided into
three categories:

(1) changes due to possible changing levels of
international trade sanctions,
(2) changes due to altering racial discrimina-
tion barriers to economic opportunity, and
(3) changes necessitated by forming a majority
government with new constituencies and new priorities.

Several problems of development may also be
delineated:

(1) problems resulting from rapid population
growth and the efforts directed toward the achievement of a more balanced distribution of income,
(2) problems of sustaining agricultural growth,
and
(3) problems of maintaining satisfactory rates
of capital formation after the transition to majority
rule.

DIOSIM was designed to assess some of these
economic growth and distributive changes. (Hereafter,
the Rhodesian DIOSIM application will be referred to
as ZIMSIM for Zimbabwian simulation.) The growth
and then reduction in trade sanctions are likely to
have the effect of cutting transport cost for imports
and exports and ultimately reducing the dependence
of high cost import substitutions. The reductions
or even termination of racial barriers to economic
opportunity will likely induce sharp changes in
agriculture; reducing modern agricultural output as
subsistence farmers take over European lands, and
European farmers and others migrate. Also, the rate
of migration from rural to urban areas can be
expected to increase.
The process of adapting government to the needs
of the majority can be expected to cause an increase
in the wages of lower income households and higher
tax rates on profits and retained earnings. The
probable decline in direct taxes as a result of
majority rule will no doubt have to be offset by increases in indirect taxes. The process of assessing
trade-offs between rapidly evolving priorities for
growth, income distribution, employment and level of
technology can utilize simulation methodologies.
ZIMSIM was designed and run for four distinct
Rhodesian patterns: (1) a base case, (2) a mild

case, (3) a severe case, and (4) a severe case which reflects strenuous efforts on the part of the new government to limit deficit and the demand for imports. The severe-constrained case, (4), focuses on the effects of strong International Monetary Fund pressures to avoid unmanageable foreign obligations.

The base year chosen was 1971, with 1972 data used to estimate difference equations. Following that initial positioning of the simulation, limited policy information is supplied to the model for the years 1973 through 1985. The 1973 through 1975 data are derived from public statistics and the model was calibrated over these years to assure reliability. Following 1975, the same growth trend is continued. Disturbances are then introduced and compared to the base run to reflect the changes of transition and the requirements of development to 1985.

To assist in visualizing the effects of the simulation changes, two tables are presented below. Figure 3.3 shows the links between broad categories of change and the twelve perturbations induced in the model to reflect the change. Figure 3.4 gives an overview of the four cases simulated. Both tables illustrate the interactive nature of the changes which reflect the complex patterns of transition and development facing Rhodesia.

Figure 3.4 gives an overview of the methods and extent of changes in the model to reflect the different situations that were anticipated as a result of transitional and development problems. The first three changes (1-2-3) are shifts in policy parameters of the model to reflect agricultural changes. The transport change (4) is an effort to show the results of the transport efficiency improvements due to the lifting of the embargo. Perturbation (5) reflects the dropping of racial barriers to urban residence. Six (6) reflects the estimated 1977 and 1978 departures of Europeans from Rhodesia during the policy analysis application of the model early in 1977. Seven (7) is the probable real wage increases that will follow from government and private efforts to affect a redistribution of income. Corresponding to the wage increase is the drop in profits (8) and retained earnings (9). Indirect taxes (10) would be expected to increase as the government attempts to generate revenues to pay for the wage increase and maintain revenues. Eleven (11) would be the result of efforts to limit foreign debt and balance of payments problems in the last case where foreign loans are limited. Perturbation (12) represents the effects of reducing the marginal efficiency of capital to show the decline

Element of Model Altered to Reflect Each Change (Read down column of each change to see how the change is input into model.)	Transitional			Developmental		
	Trade Sanctions	Racial Barriers	Governance	Pop Growth & Income Distribution	Agricultural Growth	Capital Formation
1. Agricultural exports	✓	✓		✓	✓	✓
2. Balance between TRAD and MODAG	✓	✓		✓	✓	
3. MODAG efficiency		✓		✓	✓	✓
4. Import transport costs	✓					
5. Urban drift		✓		✓		
6. Emigration of upper income households		✓	✓		✓	✓
7. Wages		✓	✓	✓		✓
8. Profits			✓	✓		✓
9. Retained earnings			✓	✓		✓
10. Indirect taxation			✓			✓
11. Government consumption			✓			
12. Capital efficiency						✓

Figure 3.3   Categories of Historic Change and Concomitant Model Changes

Perturbations	Base Case	Mild Case	Severe Case	Severe Case With Constrained Foreign Debt
1. Reduced Agri. Exports	no change	up to 25% reduction	up to 35% reduction	up to 35% reduction
2. Demand Shift from MODAG to TRAD	no change	10% shift	10% shift	10% shift
3. Reduced MODAG Efficiency	no change	no change	no change	15% reduction
4. Reduced Import Transport Costs	no change	7% & 5% reduction	7% & 5% reduction	7% & 5% reduction
5. Increased Urban Drift from 6% to	no change	7-10-6 (These are sequences of yearly change.)	7-10-8-7-6	7-10-8-7-6
6. Emigration of Upper Income Households	no change	10-15%	15-20%	15-20%
7. Wage Increases	no change	10%-10%	10%-10%	10%-10%
8. Profits Reduced to	no change	.64, .64	.28, .28	.28, .28

Figure 3.4 Description of the Differences Between the Four Simulated Cases

Figure 3.4 (continued)

Perturbations	Base Case	Mild Case	Severe Case	Severe Case With Constrained Foreign Debt
9. Reduced Retained Earnings	no change	no change	.875, .75	.875, .75
10. Increased Indirect Taxes	no change	no change	1.125	1.125
11. Cut Govt. Consumption	no change	no change	25%	25%
12. Reduced Capital Efficiency	no change	limited	severe	severe

in efficiency that transfer of management might
induce.

The base run is quite likely a political impossibility, but it is designed as an economically
stable benchmark which can be used in comparison and
definition of the mild, severe and severe-constrained
cases. In the base case, the major trends of Rhodesia
were allowed to operate with 1976 policies through
1985. A 4.4% growth rate was "planned" for the period
from 1973 to 1985 and prices were held at 1976 levels.

Future utilization of the ZIMSIM model would
require updating of scenarios and data inputs. It
would also allow more time from the 1970-71 base and
difference equations year to calibrate the model and
test its sensitivity to the experience of the economy
after the start-up years. A useful action would be
to apply the meta-model approach to sensitivity study
developed by Pook [16] to better understand the performance of the system and the linkage between policy
variables and outcome or performance variables.

The ZIMSIM Results - The ZIMSIM analysis was
made early in 1977 and therefore some of the scenarios
and conclusions may already be unfeasible. However,
the results are reported here because they do provide
insight into the character and dimension of DIOSIM
analysis. Four simulation cases were designed to
provide comparisons for contingency planning. The
base case is probably a political impossibility.
The mild and severe cases yield levels of foreign debt
that may not be supportable. Therefore, the severe-
constrained case becomes the most valuable simulation
for providing relevant analysis.

The results of the simulations are reported in
two ways. First, Figures 3.5 and 3.6 show the expected trends of GNP and per capita GNP for 1976-85.
The four cases, base, mild, severe, and severe-
constrained are reported on each graph. The second
form of reporting shows the expected percentage departures from the base case for the mild, severe,
and severe-constrained cases.

The trends of GNP, both total (Figure 3.5) and
per capita (Figure 3.6), reveal that the impact of
the world recession in 1975 may well have a continuing effect through 1978: this is most evident
in the base case on Figure 3.6. Thereafter, the
Rhodesian economy would, in the politically impractical
base case, continue to grow at a modest rate. The distribution of income in the base case appears to be
unacceptable, so the post-transition cases are more
interesting. The severe-constrained case suggests
that per capita GNP will drop by about 22% over the
decade after majority rule.

57

Figure 3.5 Trend of GNP (1976 Prices)

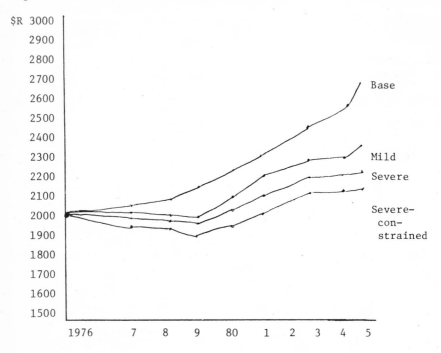

Figure 3.6 Trend of GNP per Capita (1976 Prices)

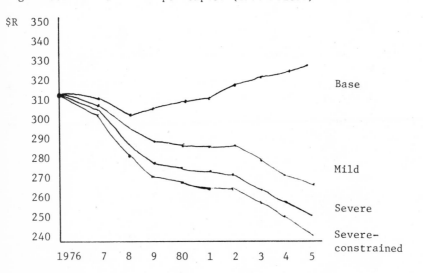

Figure 3.7

Changes in the Trend of GNP

1979			1984		
mild	severe	severe-constrained	mild	severe	severe-constrained
-8%	-10%	-12%	-14%	-18%	-22%

Although Figures 3.5 and 3.6 above give a more detailed picture, it is useful to compare the departures from the base case for 1979 and 1984. Clearly, the severe-constrained case shows the most significant decline. The changes will likely affect upper income people more adversely than lower income households.

Figure 3.8

Changes in Employment Trends

1979			1984		
mild	severe	severe-constrained	mild	severe	severe-constrained
-11%	-15%	-15%	-15%	-20%	-26%

The declines in the employment levels from the base case are significant. However, these figures are put into perspective when the Figure 3.9 figures of the proportion of the population engaged in wage employment are examined. The U.S. proportion is approximately 36%; in contrast, Figure 3.9 shows the Rhodesian proportion in the base case to be 16.4% in 1979, and 17.4% in 1984. Because a smaller part of the population is wage dependent, Figure 3.8 declines in employment are less critical.

Figure 3.9

Percentage of Population Engaged in Wage Employment

1979

base	mild	severe	severe-constrained
17%	15%	15%	15%

1984

base	mild	severe	severe-constrained
17%	15%	15%	14%

The post-transition economy of Rhodesia will inevitably need additional external assistance to recoup
the lost economic growth.

Figure 3.10

Changes in the Trends of Urban Poor

1979			1984		
mild	severe	severe-constrained	mild	severe	severe-constrained
-1%	+16%	+19%	+4%	+21%	+24%

The simulation patterns the urban drift problem
by applying a migration rate to the rural population
moving to urban areas. In the past, this migration
has been regulated and inhibited to only 5% per year.
During the immediate post-transition years, it is
expected that this rate will jump and then later
return to present levels. The number of the lowest
income urban households is a function of urban drift
and the rate of urban job formation.

The number of urban poor is expected to be
232,000 households in the base case by 1979. This
presents a very serious social and political problem.
In addition, the number is expected to grow to
359,000 by 1984: that is, one-fifth of all Rhodesian
households will be among the urban poor. The problem
of transition and the need to develop a new basis for
sustaining capital formation are such that in the

severe-constrained case, over 25 percent of all
households are expected to be among the urban poor.
Clearly, a priority effort should be considered for
urban job formation as well as activities that will
reduce urban drift pressures.

Figure 3.11

Changes in the Trends of Productive Capacity

mild	severe	severe-constrained		mild	severe	severe-constrained
-16%	-17%	-22%		-15%	-15%	-20%

Capacity appears to be a constraint only in the
severe-constrained case in 1979. A comparison of GNP
(Figure 3.7) and capacity shows that capacity is
expanding at a greater rate than GNP for the other
cases in 1979. In 1984, the GNP and capacity appear
to deviate equally from the base case figures.

Figure 3.12

Changes in the Trend of Capital Formation

mild	severe	severe-constrained		mild	severe	severe-constrained
-6%	-7%	-25%		-15%	-15%	-34%

The present structure of the Rhodesian economy
provides a strong capital formation process. This
will change with transition to majority rule. Whether
the economy will be able to retain earnings and re-
invest savings as efficiently as in the past is open
to question. The effects of constrained capital
spending in an attempt to reduce the balance of payments gap are shown in Figure 3.12. This point will
be discussed again in relation to Figure 3.15.

Figure 3.13

Changes in the Trend of Retained Earnings

1979			1984		
mild	severe	severe-constrained	mild	severe	severe-constrained
-4%	-6%	-37%	-10%	-12%	-44%

In the severe-constrained case, reliance upon retained earnings will have to diminish. Government investment will be necessary to compensate for this change.

Figure 3.14

Changes in the Trend of Savings

1979			1984		
mild	severe	severe-constrained	mild	severe	severe-constrained
-12%	-17%	-22%	-10%	-17%	-27%

The decline in savings is not expected to be as severe as the decline in retained earnings, but the combination of these two factors will cause private domestic investment to decline radically.

Figure 3.15

Comparison of Government Deficit
(in millions of Rhodesian dollars)

		1979	
base	mild	severe	severe-constrained
-16.5	-54	-66	-27

		1984	
base	mile	severe	severe-constrained
-32	-101	-120	-18

The combined effects of the severe-constrained case force government deficit to maintain levels comparable to deficit levels in the base case.

Figure 3.16

Comparison of the Balance of Payments
(in millions of Rhodesian dollars)

base	mild	1979 severe	severe-constrained
-109	-85	-107	-80

base	mild	1984 severe	severe-constrained
-129	-369	-341	-253

Figure 3.16 reflects the most critical problem facing the new government. The extreme balance of payments problem associated with the mild and severe cases make them untenable. For this reason, the severe-constrained case becomes the relevant analysis.

The heavy reliance on intermediate imports ties the development of the economy to increased foreign exchange earnings. With declining agricultural exports, the gap will grow. Strong constraints on government spending and concentrated emphasis on public and private capital formation will be needed to hold down demand for imports.

Conclusion of the ZIMSIM Study

The Rhodesian economy has been suppressing serious problems under white rule; some of the most critical are:

1. The modern, and largely white-controlled, agricultural system has been subsidized, while traditional agriculture has been taxed slightly.

2. The rate of urban drift has been artificially inhibited by limiting African mobility.

3. Rapid capital formation by Europeans has been made possible by a wage and income policy that has been extremely disadvantageous to Africans.

4. The educational system has not fostered the development of a technically competent African population.

The objective of the transition to majority rule is to eliminate these constraints. The make-up of the new government is uncertain, but the coalition that emerges will probably embark on a program to correct this social injustice; such a program will carry a high economic price tag. The large number of urban unemployed and the overwhelming increase in foreign debt stand out as severe detrimental consequences of the transition.

The rate of job formation will lag behind the growth in the numbers of people looking for work. This is a problem common to many less developed countries, but the abruptness with which Rhodesia will confront the problem is unusual, and will tend to exacerbate the problem.

Changes in income policy to assure more demand for products with a low import content seem to be desirable. Such policies would foster social goals, expand employment, and reduce import demand.

External assistance may be required to ease transitional displacement, foster development, and absorb the shock due to balance of payments problems. Transition will require training and management development programs for many industrial and agri-cultural activities. The utility and mining sectors, with modest support, are the only sectors likely to continue on a strong growth path. Other sectors (such as manufacturing, modern agriculture, con-struction and distribution) will need massive manage-ment development programs, unless the Europeans elect to stay and follow a pattern similar to that of Europeans in Kenya. This would delay transition, but sustain gross product. The type of program needed will be dependent to some extent upon the organiza-tional policies followed presently by European businessmen and the speed with which they train Africans. The traditional agriculture system is now somewhat stunted; transition will bring need for new infrastructure to supply inputs, technical assistance, and market output.

These transitional requirements will merge into development programs as the initial social justice needs are satisfied. It will then be clear that Rhodesia faces development problems similar to many

other African nations. Exports of mineral products
will help close the balance of payments gap, but the
nation will need to curb the demand for imports. At
the same time, job opportunities will have to be
provided for a rapidly expanding and urbanizing population.

As of this writing, it is not clear what the
future will bring to Rhodesia. The most valuable
contribution of this work may well be in the flexibility to allow new and presently unknown "cases"
to be assessed. As events unfold, more precise
estimates of change can be made and then perhaps
new and more useful simulations can be run. In this
way, contingency planning can be continuously updated.

Generalizations from the Rhodesian Modeling Exercise

This chapter has presented a description of the
DIOSIM model and has described application of the
model to the Rhodesian economy. History may show
that the Rhodesian scenarios chosen in early 1977
were unrealistic, but a flexible tool for analysis
of that situation now exists and as the situation
changes, new analysis could be provided.

However, this application is presented only as
an example of model use, and for our purposes here
the specific content of the analysis is not critical.
The essential conclusion is that DIOSIM can be used
to provide valuable insights into trade-off assessment and policy making. In areas of tension and
significant change, as Southern Africa, modeling
efforts can help evaluate change and direct it toward
more equitable socio-economic patterns. Furthermore,
careful public use of modeling techniques can provide a broad base of understanding for policies and
their trade-offs, thereby increasing participation
in the decision-making process and enhancing public
support of the conclusions.

The simulation modeling effort in Rhodesia
would have been strengthened by a coordinated study
of the major life support systems as was done in
Lesotho. Both parameter estimates and scenario design would have been enhanced. The requirements
and advantages of integrated life support system
studies and simulation modeling is the subject of
the next chapter.

IV. Integration of Channel Mapping and DIOSIM Techniques

Chapters II and III presented two separate methodologies for research and planning--sectoral channel mapping and DIOSIM modeling. Case studies of these applications were described and continued work with the individual techniques was suggested. This chapter attempts to integrate elements from both techniques and to show that if they are viewed as complementary, the results of combined analysis will be more beneficial than separate applications. This discussion of the integration of the two techniques is divided into four sections: history, hierarchies of life support systems, method for integration, and potential gains of integration.

The initial section, on the history of combined channel mapping and simulation techniques, describes preliminary work in Latin America that began to define the need for complementary techniques of this sort. This work was done by Charles Slater when he was the director of the Latin American Studies Center at Michigan State University. It focused interest on the shortcomings of sectoral mapping studies when used in the planning process.

Section II discusses the hierarchy of needs in all human societies. This discussion does not attempt to be exhaustive, but rather explores the problem of relating food system channel mapping (as done in Lesotho) to broader descriptive work of mapping channels of the major life support systems of any society. In this way, the concept of channel mapping is broadened to present a more comprehensive view of the entire socio-economic system. In addition, Section II discusses the distinction between life support systems and life fulfillment systems and describes how this distinction can facilitate application of the complementary techniques of channel

67

mapping and simulation modeling.

The specific technical procedure for coordinating these research approaches is developed in Section III. The process is shown to be iterative and interactive, with each technique contributing to the substance of the other.

In the final section, some of the potential benefits of the coordinated approach are discussed in terms of the issues facing Southern Africa.

History of Combined Channel Mapping and DIOSIM Techniques

In 1964, a series of studies on the role of marketing in the development of some Latin American communities began at Michigan State University. These studies focused on food marketing and grew from Slater's recognition of food systems as critical sectors of all societies, particularly technologically underdeveloped societies. Parallel to these interests were Harold Riley's research concerns about small holder agriculture and the input and output marketing institutions serving small farmers in Latin America.

Combined work began with exploratory visits to Colombia supported by grants from the Ford Foundation [18]. The conceptual framework for the research was developed and applied to several communities. The essential features of the design were to investigate food intake and purchasing behavior of a sample of urban and rural households. The inquiry would investigate both types, quantities and prices of food, and also consumer attitudes about the food system - reliability, risk, uncertainty, and information. Demographic data was also gathered. The research design then applied similar survey techniques to channel participants upstream through retailers, wholesalers, processors, assemblers, producers and input suppliers.

The combined studies then addressed the question of identifying ways in which the system could be made more efficient, and less costly in risk and uncertainty. The acceptability of changes in the technology of inputs and output marketing was also considered. There were problems of procedure because it was not always practical to sequence the surveys to fit the logic of the overall conceptual framework, but care was exercised to avoid respondent and sampling bias. The results were published to assure government, public, and foreign donor and lender appreciation of the issues of trade-offs, associated with enhancing the food system through marketing channel alterations.

In field projects in Brazil [23] and Bolivia
[21], simulation models were developed to assist
in evaluating the trade-offs between reduced food
prices and labor displacement due to technological
and systems changes in market channels. Since these
trade-offs involved both direct and indirect consequences, a simulation of the economy was needed.
However, in both cases, the models developed the food
channels rather elaborately, and the rest of the
economy was simulated as rudimentary in structure.
These projects were completed in the late 1960's.
In the Brazilian study, the results were useful to
SUDENE (Superintendent of Development in the Northeast) and development projects were designed to
implement aspects of the study. Regrettably the
President of Bolivia, General Barrientos, was killed
in an aircraft accident and the change in government
pre-empted any opportunity for timely application of
the findings. The Puerto Rican case study was done
as a benchmark rather than as a development project,
so no significant policy analysis was attempted.
Later, an agricultural marketing study of the Cauca
Valley region of Colombia was conducted by Harold
Riley [16]. However, the frame of reference for that
study was substantially different than those done as
joint projects of Slater and Riley.

In Brazil, food channel mapping and exploration
of technology transfers were conducted. These included study of supermarkets with low priced marketing of leader staple products and coordinated wholesaling channels to cut the costs of many products,
particularly the leader items. A simulation model
of the economy of the Northeast of Brazil was utilized
to evaluate these market coordination parameters,
information system improvements, and investment opportunities. Trade-off modeling became an integral part
of the food system research.

Subsequent to the completion of this work in
1970, there was no effort to continue research efforts
with combined descriptive research of market channels
and closed systems computerized simulation modelling
of the same community. In large part, the cessation
of this coordinated work reflected the recognition
that food system simulation models were focused too
narrowly and a more balanced general systems model
was needed. Interest in food system problems did not
erode; the Lesotho study was appropriately focused
upon the food system problem as a critical issue to
the community. But there are other critical life
support systems in every community and these should

also be mapped carefully. By meshing a series of
such studies, an overall simulation model can be
parameterized to assess the primary and secondary
impacts of strategies in each sector.

Hierarchies of Life Support Systems

The studies in Brazil and Puerto Rico were
initially concerned with the food system of those
nations. The studies underscored the fact that although food ranks high on the hierarchy of community
needs, the food system is only one component of the
overall social system. Investigating other needs and
the systems for fulfilling them is also essential to
providing a full description of any society.
Drawing upon the profound taxonomic contribution
of Abraham Maslow [11], a sketch of some of the major
human priorities and their corresponding socio-economic
systems can be suggested:

Priorities	Socio-Economic Systems
Security	Military, Police, and Justice Systems
Nutrition and Water	Food and Beverage Systems
Shelter	Housing
Warmth and Cover	Clothing
Health and Sani- tation	Medical Sciences
Education	Schools and Training Programs
Mobility	Transportation
Aesthetics	Art and Environmental Preser- vation Systems

Nutrition is considered one of the highest priorities
on the Maslowian hierarchy and it is significantly
interdependent with health and sanitation, and
aesthetics. The food system is the mechanism for
achieving the nutrition priority and thus minimizing
the incidence of disease, but in most societies it
also serves aesthetic and ritual functions. The
great potlatches of the Kwakiutl indians of the
American Northwest are an example of this. They
provided a ceremonial opportunity for chiefs to con-
firm their prestige by sharing huge quantities of
food and redistributing immense material wealth.
As an integral element of the potlatch, food ful-
filled ritual and aesthetic expectations of the
community. In a similar manner, food provides a means
of celebration for many occasions in modern societies.
Weddings, births, and deaths are all marked by cere-
monies that include the ritual and aesthetic

presentation of food.

Although there is general recognition that a
hierarchy exists, the ordering of priorities may vary.
As opportunities expand beyond the most primitive life
situation, the lower priorities become more important,
absorbing an increasingly greater share of resources.
For our purposes here, the precise ordering of the
hierarchy is not crucial. The point is that food
systems are one component of the overall social
system, and to provide a full description of the
society, so that policy decisions can be fully
analyzed, the other components must also be investigated. In fact, work is being planned now to explore
the feasibility of similar approaches to assess the
consequences of alternative educational policies.
One useful study in this area is the doctoral thesis
of Edward Lyell [10].

It should be pointed out that this hierarchy of
life support needs is paralleled by a hierarchy of
life fulfillment needs. The quality of life needs
are more difficult to define and vary significantly
from culture to culture, but they are closely related
to the life support priorities. In many instances,
there is considerable overlap between the two categories: food fulfills both the life support need of
nutrition and also contributes to the quality of
life in terms of aesthetics, rituals, and traditions.
Clothing is necessary for warmth and cover, but it
also affects style, status and tradition. In fact
most of the critical life support needs are closely
interwoven with a pattern of expectations that contribute to the quality of life.

Each culture has unique life fulfillment rituals
and other patterns of behavior that structure and
limit the acceptable life support activities. Certain
policies that might enhance the achievement of life
support goals may be forbidden by the culture's
quality of life standards. For example, the Hindu
peasants' refusal to eat meat would negate the
effectiveness of a policy that recommended slaughter-
ing cattle to alleviate rural hunger in India. In a
similar manner, the United States consumer fetish for
beef would inhibit a policy that sought to establish
soy analogs as the major protein source in the American
diet. Therefore it is critical that channel mappings
consider the customs and expectations of the life fulfillment hierarchy as well as the needs of the life
support hierarchy.

Moreover, no society works to achieve a high
standard on one priority before addressing the next.
All communities address all the life support tasks

71

and all the quality of life goals simultaneously and continuously. Therefore, the systems and policies affecting them are interdependent. This underscores the importance of conducting concurrent channel mapping studies in order to derive a comprehensive picture of the socio-economic system.

It is useful to see institutions and activities in relation to the holistic need satisfaction process rather than as ends in themselves. If one looks at a need and the related system for maximizing satisfaction of that need, without examining inter-related needs and the priorities for satisfying them, then suboptimal maximization occurs. A colleague, Kenneth Boulding, once said that the true name of the devil was not Beelzebub, but suboptimal maximization [1]. Using the DIOSIM framework to coordinate a series of channel mapping studies can help avoid this fragmentation.

Method for Integrated Application of Channel Mapping and DIOSIM Techniques

The motivation for integrating channel mapping and simulation modeling is clear. The techniques are complementary and each can add dimension to the analysis of the other. The benefits of such coordinated efforts will be far-reaching. However, the process for integrating these two techniques is complex. It must be interactive and iterative, with each method contributing to the substance of the other.

Figure 4.1 presents a graphic representation of the integration. It is an iterative process whereby both channel mapping and DIOSIM modeling interact to enhance the ways in which development plans are designed, presented, and evaluated comparatively. The chart also suggests that the integration of these two techniques could help redefine the decision-making group to include persons other than the historically dominant elite.

Figure 4.1 shows two parallel research programs. Each would be conducted by separate agencies and each would proceed toward its own goals. However, the programs would be carefully coordinated. The simulation work would probably be conducted under the auspices of the central planning unit of the government. The channel mapping efforts would be centered in the various government agencies that are now responsible for elements of the major life support systems. Thus the unit of government that must construct a balanced, comprehensive plan of development would have direct access to the trade-off assessment capabilities of

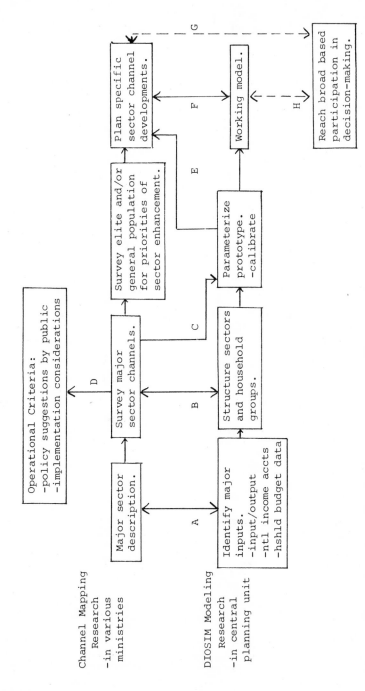

Figure 4.1   Method for Integrating Channel Mapping and DIOSIM Modeling
(Letters denote paths of interaction which are described in text.)

DIOSIM. The various ministries that are responsible
for sector plans would be directly involved in the
channel mapping research. The two research methods
are independent, but ideally they would be undertaken
simultaneously to enhance cooperation between technicians at all levels. Both arms of research must be
carefully coordinated and continued interaction between responsible parties is essential.

An alternative method of execution would involve
impartial international research teams, perhaps under
the auspices of the United Nations. This structure
could be utilized by rapidly changing governments and
could be designed to fill the vacuum created by civil
strife, outmigration, or a lack of technical experts
in the host country. The research could be centered
at a local university and thus help develop the research capability within the nation. The coordination
of a project undertaken by international agencies
would be difficult. There would be a strong tendency
for the research to gather its own momentum and fail
to be integrated into the planning process of the
host country. However, the structure is mentioned
here because the comprehensive nature of Southern
African transition suggests that although research
to facilitate planning will be desperately needed,
the lack of governmental continuity may preclude the
possibility of government sponsored research.

Each of the two parallel research programs de-
picted in Figure 4.1 follows its own steps to completion. The boxes of activity indicate that channel
mapping begins with the determination of which sectors
are to be investigated. It then proceeds to the
design and execution of the surveys which produce
certain operational criterion for consideration. Next
surveys are conducted to determine the priorities of
the elite and/or the general population. Finally,
sector plans are derived from the information and
priority base. DIOSIM modeling begins with the identification of the major data inputs to the model.
Study of these sources and of data from channel mapping
surveys will delineate the structuring of sectors and
household groups. Then the model can be parameterized
and the prototype can be tested and calibrated to
produce a working model. The horizontal arrows on the
chart indicate the sequence of events within each
method. The vertical arrows, which are labeled from
A through H for easy reference, are paths of interaction and indicate the flow of information between
the two research methods. Each of these paths will
be discussed below.

Path A operates between the initial steps of each research program. This interaction develops a specification of research needs. Information flows along the path to produce a determination of what sectors to map and what data is necessary for the parameterization of DIOSIM. Problem areas within the sectors indicate where there are policy deficiencies. Both programs of research should then concentrate efforts in these sectors. Sector boundaries should be defined that are common to both programs. It is particularly important that the sectors of special policy interest be individuated in the DIOSIM model. For instance, when DIOSIM was applied to study the 1976-78 drought in the state of Colorado, it was determined that the agriculture sector would be significantly affected by the constraints of drought and the policy instituted to cope with the problems. Since Colorado has three major types of agriculture - irrigated, dry land, and livestock - each of these varieties became a sector in the model's input/output transactions table. For other applications, however, this disaggregation would not be as useful. If the COLOSIM model is used to evaluate issues of energy use, development, and conservation in Colorado, then it is likely that agriculture should be combined as one sector and utilities and transportation should be disaggregated. The flow of information along path A can help determine policy direction and thus data needs.

The design of objective criterion of evaluation is another subject of concern along path A. In order to target and evaluate policy, it is necessary to agree upon a standard of performance. This standard may affect sector and household boundaries in DIOSIM and it will certainly help determine the form of the surveys in channel mapping. In fact, complete sections of the survey will change depending upon what criteria are devised: the survey may need to investigate nutritional status, or levels of crime, or educational achievement. Therefore, it is important that the design of objective criteria occur early in the research process and that both research teams are satisfied with the criteria chosen.

In summary, information flows in both directions along path A. An interactive process of choice and definition is needed. The research programs should develop common sectors of study and a recognition of potential policy deficiencies. The determination of objective criteria for judgment of performance should help the researchers in both programs to focus on related goals. The interaction along path A should

establish patterns of cooperation between the two
research programs. It should develop a mutual understanding and coordination. It is essential that both
groups recognize the synergistic effects of the integration of the two programs.

As the channel mapping project moves into the
survey phase of its research, the DIOSIM team begins
to structure sectors and household groups. The information flows along path B are preliminary data in
the form of boundaries, orders of magnitude, and
relevant considerations in the structuring of DIOSIM
and the design of the surveys. This could include
more information about the choice of sectors for the
input/output table. For example, in the Rhodesian
modeling exercise, survey considerations would have
led to the recognition that a mining sector needed
to be added to the original DIOSIM configuration in
order to accurately reflect the dynamics of the
Rhodesian economy. Also the preliminary results of
channel mapping could lead to adjustments in the
structuring of influences on households. For example,
KENSIM had a mechanism for monetary transfers to rural
households from the extended families residing in urban
areas. In Kenya, this was a common household income
pattern. However, when work began on the USSIM model,
it was recognized that this practice was not prevalent
in the United States, but that transfer payments to
households from government (in the form of Social
Security, disability benefits, veterans benefits, for
example) were common. Therefore, the model's structure
was altered to reflect this pattern. Results from
the pilot surveys could be utilized to initiate this
kind of change.

The definition of household categories also
flows along path B. Choices concerning model structure need to be made in terms of preliminary channel
mapping results. Presently DIOSIM categorizes households by income level and urban/rural location. However, there might be other household characteristics
that would be relevant and responsive to probable
policy. Perhaps in certain applications, age, racial
characteristics, or family size might be critical
considerations. These categories should be chosen
and defined in terms of critical policy issues and
available data. Path B provides an interactive
opportunity for selection and definition.

Sector boundaries will also be finalized as a
result of the information flows along path B. The
aggregation of the DIOSIM input/output table will
be determined and decisions will be made concerning
the sector placement of products and services.

Sector responsibilities and participation often appear
to be a well-defined aspect of the ministry divisions
within government. Accepted practice can serve as
guidelines for the DIOSIM aggregation, but frequently
DIOSIM structuring will uncover areas of ill-defined
jurisdiction and duplication of effort. For example,
petroleum processing could be considered part of the
utilities sector or the mining sector, and it certainly has significant influence on the transportation
sector. Frequently the ministry authority for a product of this kind will be diffuse also. By asking
exacting questions concerning sector aggregation,
DIOSIM can point to areas of potential confusion.

Closely related to the issue of sector aggregation is the subject of cross-elasticities, and these
also need to carefully be defined in the DIOSIM
structure. In terms of demand, certain processing
sectors exhibit a dependence on one another. For
example, if an economy produces non-ferrous metals in
great quantity, then the demand and production of
ferrous metals might be minimized. The products of
one processing sector will be substituted for the
products of another if they are available. Cross-
elasticities complicate the aggregation of the input/
output table by making certain transactions dependent
upon others. In the DIOSIM configuration, two
mechanisms have been devised to minimize the effect
of cross-elasticities: the input/output table is
disaggregated only to a minimal number of sectors,
and a market channel aggregation is used. In the
first instance, the design of robust sectors keeps
most of the cross-elasticities within one sector.
Thus in the example above, the production of both
ferrous and non-ferrous metals would be placed in
the manufacturing sector and so the effects of the
cross-elasticity would be maintained within the
sector boundary. The market channel aggregation
of DIOSIM serves a similar function. Since consumers
can purchase goods directly from only a limited
number of sectors, the model channels consumer demand
through these. In the Rhodesian model, commerce,
services, utilities, government and the traditional
sector comprise the sales component. This aggregation
minimizes the effect of cross-elasticities because
consumer demand is not generally variable between
these sectors. That is, demand for utilities cannot
be satisfied easily with services. Thus there are
mechanisms for minimizing the effects of cross-
elasticities in DIOSIM. In the applications thus far,
this has been an adequate solution. However, it must
be noted that this issue may become a greater problem

in other applications. Therefore, the preliminary
data flows along path B should investigate this issue
and the definitions of cross-elasticities should be
developed at this juncture.

The preliminary data flows of path B will provide
a further illumination of data needs and sources.
Viewing data collection with a goal orientation such
as this will help to define data needs and collection
methods. In this way, the form of data can be tailored
to expected use and time will not be wasted in collect-
ing and analyzing data that is not relevant. In
addition, the recognition of attainable data will
enable the DIOSIM researchers to structure the model
so that the data necessary for parameterization will
be available.

In summary, the information that flows along
path B is preliminary data in general terms. It flows
in both directions and enables both research teams
to derive exacting definitions of data needs and
availabilities. The end result of the path B interaction will be the final determination of sector
boundaries and household categories.

After the general data needs and categories are
established, work can progress to parameterizing the
DIOSIM model. Path C operates in one direction only:
data flows from the completed channel mappings to
parameterize and calibrate the DIOSIM model. The
data needs of DIOSIM are surprisingly limited and
channel mapping research can provide valuable insight.
One essential category of data is consumption demand
information. The income generating sources of households - employment, wages, transfers, profits and
subsistence farming - must be carefully delineated.
In addition, income disposition patterns - consumption,
taxes, savings -- must be described. Next data concerning the processing sectors must be quantified.
Production data, investment policy, business taxes,
subsidies, interest paid, and the construction effect
of investment must all be identified. Values must
also be set for imports and exports. Government
consumption, expenditures, deficit, loans and loan
service must be derived. In addition, inflation
factors must be calculated. Finally, population
change, migration, and the number of households per
category must be input to the model.

The process of parameterization should include
the use of secondary data as well as the data
assembled by channel mapping. The model needs to be
initialized several years before the present period
to provide time for an evaluation of historic tracking. Therefore, current channel mappings will be

used to define the structures of the model, calibrate,
and define areas where data is weak and needs to be
improved. Successive channel mappings will provide
a more exact data base. However, secondary data must
be used to supplement the data that flows along path
C for parameterization of the model.

In addition to providing data for the parameterization of DIOSIM, channel mapping will provide policy
suggestions from channel participants in terms of
dissatisfaction with the performance of the channel.
It is this information that flows along path D. Since
this information does not contribute directly to the
DIOSIM technology, path D flows away from the modeling
research. However, the suggestions of channel participants can prove to be valuable policy inputs.
Particularly in areas where policy decisions are made
by small elite, the level of dissatisfaction is important in determining the minimum acceptable levels of
performance. Beyond these levels, the population
will demand radical change and thus destroy the power
base of the elite. For the elite to maintain its
control, enough wealth must be distributed so that
most people have a stake in the status quo. In this
regard, channel mapping can serve as a survey of
public opinion.

Perhaps more important than considerations of
minimal acceptable standard, the opinions of channel
participants can suggest policy and implementation
considerations. The use of farm inputs in Lesotho
serves as an example of this. Channel mapping discovered that one of the reasons why farm output was
low was the very limited use of farm inputs such as
fertilizer, adequate crop storage, pesticides, and
new stocks of seed. It was found that inputs were
used infrequently because of the farmers' lack of
funds to purchase them. One policy solution to this
dilemma could be to grant credit to farmers. In
order to assure repayment of the loans, it was
suggested that credit be provided through the market
channel in small amounts at the retail outlets. This
system would provide accountability by making the
farmer's neighbor, rather than a remote government
agency, responsible for collection of the debt. In
this way, policy recommendations were derived from
the attitudes of the farmers.

This kind of policy recommendation is targeted
at the level of operational criteria. Some of the
considerations are too micro in character to be investigated by the DIOSIM model. However, channel
mapping can suggest policies and avenues for insuring
that policy will be implemented effectively. It gives

79

an indication of the degree of interest and probable level of cooperation from channel participants. Therefore these findings of the channel mapping research should not be ignored.

Path E allows the flow of tentative feasibility results of policies. The prototype model can make preliminary evaluations of policy and illustrate critical inconsistencies. The model can help to define the points of intervention that are available to policy makers. It can clarify what policies are within the financial and political authority of the government. For example, in some economies sector investment or subsidy might be options available to government decision-makers, whereas sector takeover would be untenable. Also, the DIOSIM model can illuminate the comparative results of investment only in selected sectors.

Preliminary feasibility evaluations can also clarify sector conflicts. Since the concepts of one sector plan may be detrimental to the development of other sectors, it is important that these conflicts are recognized before the sector plans are firmly established. The compromises that are necessitated by conflict resolution should be more easily derived at this preliminary stage.

In summary, path E provides the tentative feasibility results that are an essential element in the development of a balanced policy. By illustrating financial and political constraints as well as potential conflicts between sectors, this interaction facilitates the design of feasible policies.

Path F provides the avenue for the most essential interaction and synergistic improvement to the planning process. It is here that each separate technique can make the most substantive contribution to the other. The primary purpose of paths A-E is to enhance understanding, confidence, and interaction at this level.

The interaction of path F is iterative by nature. First the specific sector development plans are converted into scenarios of model input. Next the DIOSIM model is used to assess the trade-offs of alternative policies. The assessment conclusions are then used to modify the sector plan to accommodate the trade-offs. Next the modified plans are subject to further trade-off analysis. Thus, path F represents an iterative process of revision in terms of simulated risks and trade-offs.

This process operates on three distinct levels. First, the trade-offs of limited aspects of each sector plan are evaluated. For example, the effects of heavy government investment in agriculture might be investigated as one element of the agricultural sector plan. Second, the trade-offs associated with a series of individual policies are simulated and assessed. For example, the development plan of the agriculture sector might be to increase agricultural growth by a series of activities: increased government investment in the sector, decreased taxes on the purchase and maintenance of agricultural capital, and limited migration to urban areas in an effort to keep more manpower on rural farms. The three elements of this policy will have individual as well as interactive effects. Trade-off analysis can clarify the results and perhaps point to unacceptable additive impacts. In this way, the plan can be modified in terms of altering the levels of the individual elements or substituting other more effective elements. This level of trade-off analysis will be provided for the development plans in each sector of the economy. Third, the DIOSIM model can provide analysis of the interactive effects of combining all the sector plans into one overall plan of development. Since the effects of individual plans have already been isolated, this third level of trade-off analysis should clarify the additive and countervailing impacts. Trade-off assessment is complex, but the three levels of DIOSIM analysis can provide valuable insights.

In summary, path F represents a process of policy proposal, analysis, and revision. Through this iteration, the optimal policy, with the most favorable pattern of trade-offs, is derived. Awareness of the probable results supplies a more complete information base on which to predicate policy solutions.

The dotted lines of paths G and H indicate the provisional nature of these connections. Enlarging participation in the decision process may or may not be a goal of the host government. Therefore the interaction represented by paths G and H is not an essential element of the integration of channel mapping and DIOSIM modeling. However, it may be agreed that broad participation will foster egalitarian results by diffusing the concentration of wealth and power, and contributing to the goal of distributive justice. In that case, the integrated method of research and planning described here provides two direct avenues of participation. First, citizen participation can be encouraged in the choice of sector plans and policies. The precedent for participation at this level has been set by the attitude questions surveyed in the channel mapping research. Path G suggests that these attitudes become the source of sector decisions. Second, the trade-off assessment of DIOSIM could be used as a forum for communication and broad-based participation in decision-making. A sound information base will facilitate balanced policy regardless of whether the decision-making group is a small elite or a broad-based representation of the population. A more thorough discussion of broadening participation in the decision-making process will be presented in the next section.

In conclusion, this discussion of the integration of channel mapping and DIOSIM modeling indicates that they are complementary techniques. The synergistic combination of the two methods will facilitate policy research and the policy formation process. The two programs of research should be conducted separately, under the auspices of different government agencies. The DIOSIM research should be the responsibility of the central planning unit and the channel mapping research should be centered in the various ministries. However, both programs of research should be conducted simultaneously, with continued interaction on many levels. Careful coordination of the programs will help define research needs clearly and direct each effort to the same goals.

This presentation of the method of integrating channel mapping and DIOSIM modeling is designed for researchers more than policy planning technicians. The method of integration is not a completely defined procedure. It is still being developed and experimental applications are needed. However, the potential benefits of the integration seem to warrant continued development.

In sum, the integration of channel mapping and DIOSIM modeling is an interactive and iterative process. It is complex and evolving. Furthermore, it offers a comprehensive method to derive balanced and effective policy.

Potential Gains from the Integration

The essential gain from the integration of channel mapping and simulation modeling techniques is that it will provide a comprehensive system for development planning. Channel mappings will uncover shortcomings in the performance of the system and thus suggest policy options. In addition, the mapping will enhance sensitivity of cultural issues that make certain policies counter-productive or even untenable. Policy options can then be analyzed through use of the DIOSIM model. In this way, the trade-offs and the indirect impacts of the policies will become apparent

and sector plans will be seen as one element of
the system.

The integration of these two techniques will also
provide better understanding of the socio-economic
relationships in the society. The connections between productive sectors, and their relationships
to households are explicit in the DIOSIM model. In
addition, because the model is a descriptive system
and essentially theory-neutral, it can help to illuminate the ideological biases of alternative strategies.
By clearly differentiating between policy inputs and
their probable outcomes, the DIOSIM model can indicate which sets of policies will be most conducive
to achieving the goals of the society. In this way,
the ideological foundations of the power structure
of the society can be explored.

The integration of these two techniques will also
improve communication between government officials.
By placing responsibility for the DIOSIM model in the
central government and making channel mapping the
domain of separate ministries, an iteractive pattern
will be established. The central government will require inputs from the ministries in terms of data and
scenarios suggestions. The various ministries will
know that their sectoral plans will be evaluated
comprehensively and comparatively, and this will
focus their attention on the needs of other sectors.

In addition to this interactive pattern of
activities, communication will be enhanced by the
fact that this integration provides a common frame of
reference. Socio-economic relationships will be put
in the same terms and the framework will provide
common standards of performance. Therefore technicians and policy-makers at all levels, both within
the government and outside of it, will have a common
framework for analysis.

This integrated system of policy planning will
enable government officials to avoid some mistakes
through anticipation of the results. Planning will
be based on more than a trial and error process and
policies can be evaluated in terms of overall trade-
offs and the general goals of the society.

The integration of channel mapping and simulation modeling could also provide a forum for broader
citizen participation in policy planning. Both of
these techniques for policy planning can contribute
to an improvement of the information base for government decisions. Historically high technology policy
planning methods have been used internally by central
governments. Generally the results of the surveys
of public opinion and sector plans are made public.

Annual and five year plans are published with considerable detail about sector plans and often with
results of macro models to forecast planned rates of
investment and growth. Rarely however does this
process of planning include public input into the
formulation of goals and strategies for achieving the
goals.
The combined approach suggested here requires
citizen input into the data base and the scenarios.
Citizen input is critical in the life support sector
studies. Medical and other direct measures of well-
being provide the objective measure of system performance. Household income and consumption behavior
by demographic and income class are explicit elements
of both of the techniques. However, presently the
design of the techniques does not provide for broad
participation in the scenarios chosen and the weigh-
ing of trade-offs among the scenarios on the several
performance output measures.
It would be practical to include panels of
citizens in the choice of scenario priorities and in
the evaluation of outcome preferences. Whether these
participative actions are a publicized action of
government or used to provide information to a
dominant elite, the information should assist in
policy planning. Such feedback from the citizens
would improve awareness of the welfare results of
government policy. It could also provide an indication of public support of policies. Thus, use of
citizen input could lead to more informed government.
In the present era of Southern African transition to
a significantly different balance of representation
balance between Europeans and Africans, broader
participation in decision-making would almost certainly contribute to enhanced distributive justice.
The transitions which face Southern Africa are
staggering. The balance of power in governance
threatens to shift radically toward a more representative government and perhaps past that, to a government that excludes the current power groups. Economic
change seems inevitable as the majority of the population demands a greater share of the wealth of the
region. However, these demands may force many of the
technically trained people to leave the area and
thus cause a decline in productivity and an interim
trend back toward subsistence agriculture. The social
consequences of these political and economic changes
will be overwhelming.
Planning for such sweeping changes is a difficult task. The integration of channel mapping and
simulation modeling can provide more complete

information about alternative strategies and so
help avoid the pitfalls of sudden comprehensive
changes. By anticipating the operating trends,
perhaps ameliorating strategies can be derived.
In addition, by encouraging citizen involvement in
performance evaluation and policy choice, citizen
support of the government will be enhanced. In short,
the integration of channel mapping and simulation
modeling in the planning process can perhaps help
direct Southern African transitions to a goal
orientation, rather than allowing them to occur as
a pattern of haphazard destruction.

V. Conclusions and Perspectives

This final chapter investigates new directions
for the application of channel mapping and simulation
modeling as techniques for policy planning. The
discussion begins by defining two classifications
of social science research modes and describes how the
two planning methods presented in this book fit into
the distinction. Next some general conclusions about
channel mapping and simulation modeling, and their
integration, are presented. The discussion then
proceeds to a presentation of some improvements and
developments that are needed to make these techniques
more responsive to the challenge of social planning
in times of stress. Then some brief suggestions
are made concerning continued application.
The final section of this chapter goes beyond
the usual content of concluding chapters and discusses a new perspective on policy planning. The
study of social process has become a fragmented
tradition, with many disciplines carving out their
own areas of specialization. The authors believe
that this fragmentation has seriously detrimental
consequences for policy planning. Therefore, this
final section is an attempt to illustrate how the
planning techniques that we have presented could be
used advantageously as a framework for the reintegration of social process study and planning.

Two Classifications of Social Science Research Modes

Social science research can be characterized
as micro or macro in character, and also as positive
or normative in use and design. Micro research investigates conditions, practices and needs of an
individual or firm. The social environment of the
individual is considered to be an externality and the

research focuses narrowly on one specific institution. In contrast, macro research concerns the entire society and focuses on how individual institutions fit together to form a system. It stresses the interaction between sections and frequently considers the integrated goals of the community. Positive research is descriptive. It investigates an area of interest and reports on the existing conditions. By contrast, normative research is judgmental. It seeks to evaluate current conditions and point to feasible and desirable improvements. These two sets of distinctions are not mutually exclusive: for example, macro research can be positive or normative, as can micro research. However, the failure to clearly distinguish between these classifications has led to much confusion in social science research, particularly when the research is applied to the policy formation process.

The policy formation process itself is normative. It judges what is best for the community and attempts to design ways to achieve these goals. To the extent that DIOSIM modeling is used as a tool for trade-off assessment, it is used as normative research. However, the actual design and parameterization of the simulation is descriptive in character. It is not until a decision-maker utilizes the model to make comparisons and judgments that it becomes normative. The channel mapping methodology described in this book will facilitate the policy formation process, but the character of the research itself is positive. That is, channel mapping provides a description of what is, not what ought to be. In this way, it provides a sound information base for choosing and implementing policy, as well as a benchmark for determining progress made toward achieving the goals.

This distinction between normative and positive considerations is frequently confused. The value of both varities of research is often diminished because researchers and planners fail to distinguish between the current facts of the situation, the desired goals, the means of achieving those goals and the progress made toward the goals. By clearly delineating these differences, research can be designed more effectively and utilized more efficiently in the policy formation process.

The distinction between micro and macro research also provides a comparative framework for simulation modeling and channel mapping. The descriptive research of channel mapping operates on several micro levels within the community. It investigates the needs, risks, and performance of food channel participants from producer to distributor to consumer. In turn, this micro research is integrated into a comprehensive description of how the whole sector functions. This description then becomes an element of the simulation model that describes the entire system. The simulation model and its use in the policy formation process of the community is macro in character. It concerns community wide performance of the economic sectors, and policy that will affect all members of the community. Macro performance measures include the survival of the society, nutritional status, growth and distribution of real income, and resource development and preservation. Many levels of micro institutions (such as individuals, households, regions, public service units, commercial establishments and international agencies) can both support and undercut these goals. These institutions may share the overall goals of the community but they also have private and specific goals which may conflict with the achievement of the larger goals. Complete descriptive research is needed to define the workings of each micro institution and its performance and goals. Then this research must be integrated to define the inter-relationships and interactions on the macro level.

From this brief explanation, it is clear that channel mapping research is positive and micro in character. However, it can be expanded to provide a macro description of the society and it can facilitate the normative policy formation process. DIOSIM modeling, on the other hand, is macro in character. Furthermore, it is positive yet it can be used directly for the normative purposes of policy formation.

General Conclusions about Channel Mapping and DIOSIM Modeling

Chapter II described a prototype illustration of channel mapping as a research technique that can facilitate policy planning. Chapter III described the DIOSIM model of Rhodesia as a case study of the use of simulation in policy planning. Chapter IV discussed the benefits of a combined research effort. For purposes of emphasis, this section will review the general conclusions about each technique and their combined application.

Channel mapping is a relatively quick and inexpensive technique that can provide a sound information base. It is possible to conduct a complete sector study in six months. Expenses are modest because the technique involves a low level of technology and a minimal number of technicians.

In addition to its low cost and relative speed, channel mapping can strengthen understanding of sector processes. It investigates the performance and perceived risks of channel participants. It describes the relationship between various elements of the channel. In providing a thorough description of the channel participants and mechanisms, channel mapping research suggests strategies for enhancement of channel performance. These strategies are based upon the comments of channel participants and thus they may help policy makers to design programs that will be accepted and successful.

The descriptions that are derived from channel mapping research also provide a benchmark of channel performance. They give a description of how the channel operated at one particular point in time. This benchmark can then be used as a point of comparison for evaluating change and monitoring the progress made toward achieving policy goals. Use of the channel mapping as a benchmark underscores the importance of determining objective criteria of channel performance. In the case of the food system, the criterion was nutritional status, but for other channels, different measures would need to be defined. This criterion is essential because without it there is no objective way to evaluate change.

When channel mapping research is done in an area like Lesotho, it can contribute to the research capability of the host nation. Students and faculty from the local university can be taught the method and thus a data collection and maintenance capability can be developed. This capability is important because it can enable local agencies to monitor programs and progress.

The final general conclusion about channel mapping is that several concurrent mappings can give an overview of the entire economy. The integration of several mappings can be developed into a systems analysis to describe the interaction and mutual interdependencies of the various life support systems within the society.

As shown in Chapter III, simulation modeling also provides a systems view of society. In addition to an input/output description, the DIOSIM system describes the flows of goods and funds between the producing, distributing, consuming, and governmental sectors. DIOSIM describes a complex system, yet is able to identify the responses of specific elements of this system to complex patterns of change and policy.

The results of DIOSIM models have been shown to

90

be accurate. By choosing a base year that is several years in the past, the model output can be calibrated against historic data and thus users can be assured that it is tracking before it is applied.

The data requirements of DIOSIM models are comparatively small. Unlike many simulation models that require extensive sources and manipulation, it is generally possible to parameterize a DIOSIM model from published statistics. The crucial data elements are the national income accounts of the region to be modeled, household budget surveys, and an input/output transaction table. The model can be made operational quickly and inexpensively using data from published sources. It has been pointed out that the data derived from channel mapping studies would enhance the data used in DIOSIM models, but this refinement would not necessarily detract from the relative simplicity of DIOSIM data needs.

The final conclusion about DIOSIM modeling is that it provides an operational description of the whole society that can be utilized for purposes of trade-off assessment. Thus DIOSIM models are uniquely suited to analyze the complex interactive nature of policy decisions.

The integration of channel mapping and DIOSIM modeling strengthens both techniques. In the policy planning process, these two techniques are complementary. The goal of parameterizing a DIOSIM model helps define data needs clearly and so improves the efficiency of the channel mapping technique. Channel mapping can provide accurate data for parameterizing and calibrating the model. This data can increase the policy makers confidence in the results of the model. In addition, the combined approach of channel mapping and DIOSIM modeling can increase the coordination and communication between the decision-making agencies of government. This can help planners avoid a duplication of effort and provide a stronger base for the policy implementation process.

Together channel mapping and DIOSIM modeling provide a comprehensive approach to facilitate the planning process. Channel mapping suggests strategies and provides a benchmark and objective criteria for evaluation. Modeling evaluates the interactive effects of the alternative strategies and describes the associated trade-offs.

Suggested Improvements and Developments

Channel mapping and DIOSIM modeling as described in this book are in the process of evolution. They

are not presented as complete and final techniques.
Integration of the methods, as described in Chapter
IV, is one crucial direction for synergistic improvement. However, there are also specific developments
that could improve each of the techniques separately.
The needed improvements for channel mapping are more
general so they will be described first. The discussion will then turn to possible developments for
the simulation modeling.

Since the primary data collection techniques
of channel mapping research are survey methods, the
major source of improvement is finding more effective
ways to ask questions to get the information needed.
This is an evolving task since the items of interest
are refined continually and each survey points to
ways to improve measurement technique. Two issues
that will inevitably remain points of concern are
measures of income and consumption levels in the
particular life support system studied. It is difficult to get reliable and unbiased responses concerning these issues and therefore particular attention
should be given to these areas.

Another critical area for continued improvement
in channel mapping is the definition of the objective
criterion of evaluation. For the food system research, there had been extensive study on the required
food intake for adequate nutrition. Guidelines on
intake and expected levels of growth had been established and the use of reference groups for comparison
was common practice. Therefore, the objective
criterion for that life support system was fairly
easy to establish. In other sectors, this issue will
be more difficult. It may be necessary to examine
levels of expectation and historical patterns. In
some instances the criterion may be dependent upon a
consensus of opinion within the society. Therefore,
definition of the criterion must be approached carefully.

One final area for improvement in channel mapping
is in sample design and statistical analysis of results. In the Lesotho study, the sample frames for
the household survey and the nutritional status survey
were similar, but not identical. Identical frames
would have increased the level of confidence in the
results. In addition, care must be taken in analysis
so that the results are not biased by the researchers
expectations.

In many ways, these suggested improvements in
channel mapping are no more than the standard amoni-
tion to conduct careful and accurate research. However, it seemed relevant to outline them here in an

effort to give an unbiased picture of the difficulties that might be encountered. The suggested improvements for DIOSIM modeling are more uniquely tailored to this particular technique.

The varied applications that the DIOSIM model has had encourage the authors to believe that continued development of the model would be valuable. Presently there are six areas of research and development interest: documentation, input/output balancing on an annual basis, more elaborate lags, a monetary feature, fuller use of the meta-model, and interactive developments to facilitate the utilization of the model in the policy formation process. An exhaustive discussion of each of these concepts is not warranted here, but a brief outline of each direction may be of value.

Work on the DIOSIM model has been undertaken in response to particular policy issues. This orientation necessitates rapid work and therefore the documentation of the model has not been fully developed. In order to facilitate expanded use of the model and place it more in the public domain, complete documentation is needed. This documentation should be in the form of a users' manual that explains the mechanisms and uses of the model and defines data needs, sources and methods of derivation. Work on the users' manual for the COLOSIM model is proceeding under the auspices of the Office of the Governor of the State of Colorado and it is hoped that this manual can then be generalized to provide documentation for the entire DIOSIM concept.

DIOSIM models are initially parameterized with a balanced input/output transactions table. However, the technical coefficients of change alter the I/O annually in response to changing levels of investment. In the current model configuration, the balance of the I/O is never checked after the initial period. Concern about this failing has been minimized by the fact that the model seems to track well against historic data in the first four or five years of operation. However, tests should be made to evaluate the extent and effect of imbalance that is induced, and to introduce an annual balancing routine.

The development of more elaborate lags in the capital formation process is also an area for potential model improvement. Presently in the model, investment in one year induces construction effects, capacity changes, and I/O coefficient changes in the same year. This is a simple and efficient mechanism, but it is not particularly realistic. In the COLOSIM application of the model, some experimenting with investment lags was undertaken. However, this work did

93

not produce final conclusions. The investigations
should be continued to evaluate the length of lags
and also alternative patterns of lags under different
economic conditions.

Another feature of the model that should be
examined is the simulation of stocks of money in
addition to the present system of monitoring flows.
What is needed is some way to portray the behavior of
savings and deferred income that is held in a savings
pool. Most of these funds in industrial nations go
into the stock market or into debt instruments in the
form of insurance funds, private savings, or retained
earnings. The pool of funds is subject to some speculative value shifts that are a result of future
expectations concerning prime rates due to changes in
prices as well as government spending and the expected
future demand for investments by industry. In addition, speculative value is inversely related to the
interest rate. The interest rate is largely a matter
of national monetary policy, but it is also responsive
to the demand for investment. Thus, a new monetary
feature in the model could operate as a pool drawing
funds from the distribution sub-routine. The funds
could then be applied to the investment system as the
demand for investments calls for debt financing or
new issues.

Application of the meta-model concept to fully
investigate the model's reliability and sensitivity
to complex perturbations is another avenue of model
development. Meta-model testing and evaluation was
the subject of Laszlo Pook's dissertation [16] and
this work needs to be continued. The relationship
between policy variables and key output can be examined
by subjecting the variables to experimental designs of
model runs with different parameter values for the
control variables. The resulting polynomial expressions
can provide an explicit mathematical link between
policy variables and output variables. In this way,
the sensitivity can be directly investigated and the
designers of the model can utilize the results to
review the data and underlying theory of the model.
Fuller use of the meta-model could improve the reliability and confidence level of each application
of the DIOSIM concept.

Interactive improvements to facilitate the use
of DIOSIM in the policy formation process are perhaps
the most critical areas for research and development.
Currently, input to the model is entirely in the batch
mode. This is cumbersome. At the very least, change
is needed to make the annual policy inputs accessible
from interactive terminals. This would be faster

94

and more flexible and would thus facilitate use by policy planners. Included with this interactive change, a computerized program of user instruction would be invaluable. This program could build on the users' manual concept so that varied users could confidently access the model. It would allow policy makers to experiment easily with varying levels and combinations of policy input. In addition, output on interactive terminals could use graphics and time series on selected output for easy comparison. This form of output would be more flexible than flipping through pages of print-out and pulling off critical elements for analysis.

These interactive improvements in input and output would be designed to facilitate use of the DIOSIM concept by decision-makers. Thus they are related to the larger issue of getting social science research into the mainstream of the policy formation process. DIOSIM can be used for trade-off assessment; it can present the results of various strategies and scenarios. But then the question becomes what results are acceptable. The design of objective criteria can help answer this question, but in the final analysis it comes down to the issue of what values are important to the society. The double edge of this issue is frequently overlooked, but the question is what results are acceptable and also what policy inputs are acceptable. The values of the society will affect both the means and the ends.

DIOSIM can illustrate trade-offs, but the policy decisions must be based on the decision-makers' values. The level of participation in the decision process can be broad or narrow: it can range from citizen surveys to representative government to limited ministry participation to a small elite or even one man rule. The process may involve formal or informal methods of analysis. But a clear delineation of the trade-offs will enhance the understanding of the values that the decisions reflect. Furthermore it will illuminate the logical connection between policy inputs and their outcomes. Hopefully this will contribute to the formation of optimal policy.

Further Application

Before turning to the final section on the integration of social process, a brief discussion on future work is included. New applications in individual countries are suggested as well as a regional model of Southern Africa.

Channel mapping and DIOSIM modeling are valuable techniques to facilitate the policy planning process. Therefore, their expanded application in the nations of Southern Africa could provide guidance in this era of transition. As the concluding sections of Chapters II and III pointed out, improved information can only enhance understanding of the difficult choices that face each of the communities. These techniques, both individually and as a combined effort, could help to ease what has already become a difficult transition.

But in addition to applications in individual countries, the DIOSIM concept could be used to develop a regional model of Southern Africa. Such a model would underscore the similarities between nations and differentiate the needs and constraints that operate there but not in other regions of the world. It would assist in planning for transition and development by providing users with a new method for assessing complex trade-offs associated with altered trade and labor relations and shifting social patterns. In this way, a regional model could demonstrate the mutual benefits of cooperation and combined planning. The technical, social and economic aspects of Southern Africa transition are shared by the nations of the region. A regional DIOSIM model could be an aid to defining the ground for cooperation and provide a forum for discussion.

The Integration of Social Process Study

The modern disciplines of social science have evolved over the past two hundred years from the common roots of philosophy and political-economy. Today we concentrate separately on economics, political science, psychology, sociology, anthropology or the applied disciplines of business, government, and communications. Historically this segmentation derived from the eclectic study of moral, social, and economic philosophy.

As a result of conceptual and technical developments, each of the social science disciplines can provide a rich array of descriptive research. Specialization of interest has added depth to the methods and findings of each sub-division. The focusing of subject area has made each field manageable and thus fostered the development of a level of detail that would have been impossible in the realm of general philosophy. Arranging the study of social process into concise compartments has imposed an order on the knowledge that we have cultivated.

But the specialization that we have contrived
has precluded the development of an overall view of
social process. The study, or indeed the practice,
is not seen in a comprehensive way. There is little
communication between disciplines and significant
duplication of effort exists. Specialization has
produced an intense inefficiency of tunnel vision,
with many conflicting areas failing to regroup into
an integrated system.

A profound and general consequence of the fragmentation of social process study is that many individuals who assume leadership roles in modern
society have had limited, if any, training in social
process traditions. Their perspective frequently
prohibits them from accessing broad staff support
and developing balanced policies of governance. This
trend is common to capitalist, socialist, and developing societies. The background of most of the world's
leadership is military training or legal expertise.
A limited number of leaders are trained in business
practice, and even fewer have training as academic
specialists, social scientists, or physical scientists.
We are therefore living in a period when social process
information or training plays a very limited role in
the leadership and planning of an extremely dynamic
situation.

In policy work, the fragmentation of social
process has far-reaching detrimental effects. It
tends to encourage the selective attention of decision-
makers. Therefore it fosters action in areas where
the proponents speak the loudest and have the most
familiar evidence of need. Frequently the result of
this kind of planning is a series of uncoordinated
target projects that may compete with one another
and even be counter-productive in terms of overall
societal goals.

It is when problems of profound transition in
social process are contemplated that the fragmentation becomes critically dysfunctional. In times of
intense stress, when management problems are greatest,
the lack of integration causes unmanageable conflicts
and overwhelming confusions. It appears that the
challenges confronting Southern Africa in transition
and development could best be met by the reintegration
of social process study and application.

Many of the social science disciplines are coming
to use systems analysis as the core of their investigation. This common trend could be used as a basis
for the reintegration of social process study. Systems
analysis emphasizes the whole system, and studies the
relationships and interdependencies of the component
parts.

DIOSIM is a systems model of social process.
It has several features that make it uniquely suited
to easing transition in Southern Africa. Perhaps the
most unusual aspect of DIOSIM is that it allows the
user to operate in a political-economic framework that
can reflect a range of policies. The normative policy
framework is the users' decision; that is, the DIOSIM
model is policy neutral. The policy inputs of one
governing philosophy versus another can be simulated,
and some of the welfare results can be compared.
Parameter shifts are the mechanism by which the model
accommodates policy differences, but the underlying
political basis for the pattern of annual parameter
input shifts can be described as a continuum from
capitalist through Keynesian, to Marxist doctrine.
Perhaps it is irresponsibly simplistic to attempt to
distinguish these archetypical economic theories in
terms of model inputs, but the essential differences
seem to lie along the vectors of government expenditure, profit, and wages. The capitalist theory
favors high profits, minimal wages, and low government
expenditure. Keynesian doctrine fosters high wage
and transfer payments, low profit, and significant
governmental participation. Marxist philosophy
advocates universally high wages, very low profits,
and high government investment.

These politically initiated policies can be
translated into the model parameters of government
spending (sector subsidy, transfers to households,
investment per sector, and regulations on consumer
imports), population changes, external investment,
and export policy at external world prices. Once tax
and debt policies are set, government income is not
a normative option, but rather an outcome of the
operation of the economy. The export policy by sector
is the result of policy choices that elect to export
rather than allow domestic consumption of the sector's
product. External investment may be controlled, but
once in the economy, it expands the available capital
stocks and hopefully increases output. Eventually
these effects will contribute to the expansion of
savings and investment. Government policy can influence the decision of which sectors receive investment funds. Interest payment on any return to the
external investor is also a policy decision. This
policy is usually set before external investment is
made, and if it changes radically toward reduced re-
turns then the flow of external investment will almost certainly be interrupted. Migration rate is
exogenous to the model also. In some cases the rate
of flight is important, in others in-migration deserves
study.

The DIOSIM model can evaluate the welfare consequences of alternate policy sets through an array
of measures. The most essential of the measures are
economic growth (on sectoral and national levels),
income distribution to households (both monetary and
traditional), and employment by sector and income
class. A potential measure that seems to warrant
development is resource development and preservation.
By careful evaluation of the welfare results, the
DIOSIM model delineates the benefits of conflicting
policies and underscores the difference between
normative policy and hoped for gains.

In addition to providing a theory neutral forum
for evaluating the welfare consequences of alternate
policies, DIOSIM can contribute to the integration
of social process by providing a framework of analysis.
It succinctly defines processing sectors, the
operations of government, and household income
classifications. It circumscribes the boundaries
between these components, and explains the flows and
interdependencies among them. Finally, the model
delineates the drivers for change. The framework
that is thus achieved provides a forum for enhanced
communication and mutual understanding between policy
makers.

In short, DIOSIM investigates the critical
issues of our time - economic development, population
pressures, income distribution, government growth,
employment, and resource constraints. It relates
these issues in a system that can provide a framework
for the integration of the planning process. There
is a tradition of thought that interprets planning as
a limit on freedom. But if serious, holistic planning
is not undertaken, the gravity of these issues will
conspire to make the random pattern of decision far
from optimal and less free than the carefully planned
alternative.

Figure 5.1 presents a diagram of the policy
formation process. It is necessarily simplified because no society can afford the luxury of solving
one problem at a time. In reality, the problems overlap, and the policy formation process occurs simultaneously on many levels. But if policy formation
is seen as an orderly process, in which policies
are evaluated in terms of their primary and secondary
effects, then the integration of social process will
become more apparent. The purpose of the following
discussion is to describe the policy formation
process as an ordered series of steps and then explain
how channel mapping and DIOSIM modeling can facilitate
the process and help decision makers maintain a

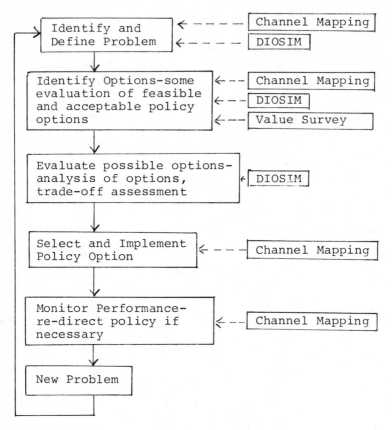

Figure 5.1   Diagram of Policy Formation Process

(Dotted lines indicate phases in which channel
mapping and DIOSIM modeling can facilitate
process.)

comprehensive view of its interactive nature.

The initial step of the policy formation process is the identification and definition of the problem. The dynamics of this process are complex even though it frequently appears that problems are obvious. Focusing problems so that they are clearly understood and responsive to solution is a difficult task. As Chapter II describes, nutritional performance was generally recognized to be inadequate in Lesotho. However, a national conference was required to define the dimensions of the problem and the degree of commitment to its solution. Furthermore, the consensus of the conference was that the nutrition problem was not fully understood and therefore research should be undertaken to examine the extent of the inadequacy. Channel mapping research was designed and performed in an attempt to define the limits of the nutrition problem. Thus, the initial step of the policy formation process may be a lengthy process in itself.

Once the problem has been identified and focused, policy makers must identify the options that would be acceptable means of solution. This aspect of the process necessitates a clear recognition of the range of feasible policy options. That is, the decision makers must understand what is within the financial means of the government and what is within its realm of political power. In addition, the identification of policy options includes some evaluation of what options would be acceptable to the populace. For example, birth control might be a way to limit the population and thus ease the nutrition problem. But if the population is morally opposed to the use of contraceptives, then the effectiveness of this option must be questioned. Since there are usually several ways to achieve the same end, the evaluation of the acceptability of the policy options themselves is critical. Channel mapping and value surveys that identify covert values can help make these evaluations by posing attitude questions and asking channel participants for suggestions of how to ameliorate problems.

In any political-economic system, permissible policies and acceptable outcomes are functions of the prevailing philosophies. Given the constraints within the system, desirable outcomes often fall short of expectations that are based on certain combinations of acceptable policy sets. Furthermore, optimal outcomes will often be the result of policy sets that outside the acceptable range. A trade-off model like DIOSIM can be utilized to illuminate the interactive connections between policy sets and outcome

101

combinations. However, the decision-maker must then use this analysis to determine desirable and feasible policies as they relate to acceptable outcomes. Frequently this is a complicated task because the decision-makers do not fully understand their values and therefore can not use them as the basis for rational decisions. Judgment analysis, in its many forms, has served to investigate and identify covert human values [6, 7]. Once these values are recognized, the search for policy/outcome combinations that satisfy the decision-makers goals can be focused.

After the range of policy options has been narrowed down to those which appear to be feasible to implement, the results of the options must be carefully analyzed. This is a difficult task because until the policies are actually implemented, assessment of the results can only be speculative. However, DIOSIM is one method to provide trade-off assessment of alternate policies. It can uncover complex interactive results that may otherwise be overlooked and it can provide insight into the secondary impacts of policy. DIOSIM will focus attention on the entire social process and thus force policy makers to consider the full effects of change. It is in this way that DIOSIM will provide the basis for the integration of social process study.

Building on the trade-off assessment of DIOSIM, a policy must be selected and implemented. The selection process will differ according to the form of government, but use of DIOSIM input could provide a forum of participation. It seems that broad participation would best foster egalitarian results. But regardless of the level of participation, knowledge of the probable consequences of policies will contribute to the goal orientation and success of the policy formation process.

Implementation is the second phase of step four in the policy formation process. In general, the mechanisms for implementation are beyond the scope of this discussion, but it can be pointed out that channel mapping will often describe points of intervention. For example, if a policy were chosen in the Lesotho case to encourage the use of fertilizer on home farms, then the farmers themselves have already indicated that small packages, distributed at local stores would be the best means of implementing the policy. Careful attention to the conclusions of channel mapping can often point to similar methods of implementation.

After the policy has been chosen and implemented and has been in operation for a time, performance must be monitored. An evaluation must be made of whether the implementation is achieving the desired goals. Because the goals have been stated clearly in step one, assessment of progress is simplified. In addition, the description produced by channel mapping research provides a benchmark for comparison and the objective criterion provides a standard of evaluation.

If evaluation against these standards indicates that the policy is not achieving the desired goals, re-direction may be necessary. Time frames may need to be altered or perhaps new policies will have to be chosen. But the monitoring of performance and evaluation of progress made are essential elements in a policy formation process that reflects the integration of social process.

In summary, the synergistic combination of channel mapping and DIOSIM modeling can provide a means for integrating social process research and harnessing that integration to help make better decisions. The challenges that face Southern Africa in this decade are staggering and it will require immense effort and dedication to meet them. It is hoped that this book will serve as a call to action.

References

1. BOULDING, Kenneth. "Fun and Games with the Gross National Product: the Role of Misleading Indicators in Social Policy." In The Environmental Crisis, edited by Harold Helfrich, Jr. New Haven: Yale University Press, 1970.

2. BURGESS, Julian. Interdependence in Southern Africa: Trade and Transport Links in South, Central, and East Africa, Special Report No. 32. London: Economist Intelligence Unit, 1976.

3. CENTRAL PLANNING AND DEVELOPMENT OFFICE. Kingdom of Lesotho Second Five Year Development Plan. Maseru, Lesotho: Government of Lesotho, 1976.

4. DAHRINGER, Lee D. Strategies for Food System Enhancement in Lesotho through New Developments in the Market Process Concept. Unpublished doctoral dissertation, University of Colorado Graduate School of Business, 1978.

5. GRUNDY, Kenneth W. Confrontation and Accommodation in Southern Africa. Berkeley: University of California Press, 1973.

6. HAMMOND, Kenneth and BREHMER, B. "Quasi-rationality and Distrust: Implications for International Conflict." In Human Judgment and Social Interaction, edited by L. Rappoport and D. A. Summers. New York: Holt, Rinehart, and Winston, 1973.

7. HAMMOND, Kenneth, STEWART, T. R., BREHMER, B., and STEINMANN, D. O. "Social Judgment Theory." In Human Judgment and Decision Processes: Formal and Mathematical Approaches, edited by M. F. Kaplan and S. Schwartz. New York: Academic Press, 1975.

8. JOHNSTON, Bruce F. and KILBY, Peter. Agriculture and Structural Transformation: Economic Strategies in Late Developing Countries. New York: Oxford University Press, 1975.

9. LINDEN, Eugene. The Alms Race: The Impact of American Voluntary Aid Abroad. New York: Random House, Inc., 1976.

10. LYELL, Edward. The Cost and Structure of Higher Education: Implications for Government Policy in Steady State. Unpublished doctoral dissertation, University of Colorado Graduate School of Business, 1977.

11. MASLOW, Abraham. New Knowledge in Human Values. New York: Harper, 1959.

12. MONTHLY DIGEST OF STATISTICS, AUGUST 1976. Salisbury: Central Statistics Office of the Government of Rhodesia, 1976.

13. MUNOZ, J. A. and ANDERSON, M. M. Basutoland Nutrition Survey 1956-1960. Geneva: World Health Organization, 1960.

14. NELSON, Harold D., et al. Area Handbook for Southern Rhodesia. Washington, D.C.: Foreign Area Studies of American University, 1975.

15. PLANNING ASSISTANCE, INC. "Report on Lesotho National Nutrition Conference, Roma, December 7-13, 1975." Maseru, Lesotho: Planning Assistance, Inc., 1976.

16. POOK, Laszlo A. A Method for Establishing Sensitivity and Reliability Measures for a Class of Simulation Models. Unpublished doctoral dissertation, University of Colorado Graduate School of Business, 1977.

17. PRATT, Graham and THORBECKE, Eric. Planning Techniques for a Better Future. Geneva: International Labour Office, 1976.

18. RILEY, Harold, KELLY, Harrison, et al. Market Coordination in the Development of the Cauca Valley Region - Colombia. East Lansing: Latin American Studies Center, Michigan State University, 1970.

19. RILEY, Harold, SLATER, Charles, et al. Food Marketing in the Economic Development of Puerto Rico. East Lansing: Latin American Studies Center, Michigan State University, 1970.

20. SEFALI, Michael, MOKHESI, Phallang, et al. An Exploratory Study of the Food System of Lesotho: A Report to the Lesotho Food and Nutrition Council. New York: Planning Assistance, Inc., 1977.

21. SLATER, Charles, HENLEY, Donald, et al. Market Processes in La Paz, Bolivia. East Lansing: Latin American Studies Center, Michigan State University, 1969.

22. SLATER, Charles, POOK, Laszlo, et al. Simulating Colorado's Drought. Report prepared for the Office of the Governor of the State of Colorado, March, 1977.

23. SLATER, Charles, RILEY, Harold, et al. Market Processes in the Recife Area of Northeast Brazil. East Lansing: Latin American Studies Center, Michigan State University, 1969.

24. SLATER, Charles, and WALSHAM, Geoffrey. "A General Systems Simulation of the Kenyan Economy." Working Paper #174, Institute of Development Studies, University of Nairobi, July, 1974.

25. SLATER, Charles, and WALSHAM, Geoffrey. "A Systems Simulation Model of the Kenyan Economy." OMEGA, The International Journal of Management Science, Vol. 3, No. 5, 1975.

26. SLATER, Charles, WALSHAM, Geoffrey, and SHAH, Mahendra. KENSIM: A Systems Simulation of the Developing Kenyan Economy 1970-1978. Boulder: Westview Press, 1977.

27. SLATER, Charles, WALSHAM, Geoffrey, et al. Rhodesian Economic Simulation, 1975-85. Unpublished report for the United States Agency for International Development, South African Desk, February, 1977. Release permission granted in letter from Thomas Quimby, Director, December 22, 1977.

28. WHITSUN FOUNDATION. A Programme for National Development. Salisbury: The Whitsun Foundation, April 1976.

29. WORLD BANK. Lesotho: A Development Challenge. Washington, D.C.: The World Bank, 1975.

30. ZERFAS, Fred and SHORR, Irwin. The Kingdom of Lesotho National Nutrition Survey. Los Angeles: University of California at Los Angeles Nutrition Assessment Unit, School of Public Health, 1976.

Appendix I

More Detail on the Rhodesian Model

Data Sources of ZIMSIM

The data sources are included in this book as an example of the character and extent of data that is necessary to operationalize a DIOSIM model.
The data sources of ZIMSIM are listed by the following decks:

Deck I   - the 1971 base year data.

Deck II   - the 1972 difference equation data.

Deck III - the 1973, 1974, 1975 simulation calibration and test data.

Deck IV   - the 1976 through 1985 policy data.

Deck I - 1971 Base Year Data

Cards 100-191: the input/output matrix of the Rhodesian economy for 1971. These are estimates of the dollar flows of inter-industry transfers for that year. The input/output was estimated by first deriving working approximations of the outlays of each sector. The traditional direct farm consumption sector was estimated initially at 91.1 million Rhodesian dollars, based on the Whitson Foundation Study [28]. (The Whitson study estimates that the income per household for rural African households in 1972 was $112 per household, cash and kind. Thus, 820,000 households would produce about 91.1 million dollars in income.) According to Table 52 of the August, 1976, Monthly Digest of Statistics [12] compiled by the Central Statistics Office, Salisbury, Rhodesia, African rural household consumption of home production was $70,700,000. According to Table 20 of that Digest [12] the sum of African and European agricultural output was estimated to be $224,700,000. Mining was estimated at $101,200,000 from Table 26. Gross output of manufacturing was estimated from Table 27 to be $757,700,000 in 1971. Building and construction, combining Tables 31 and 39, were estimated to be $115,800,000. Utilities were estimated from the production figures of 3.7 million kilowatt hours produced in 1971 at $17.56 per kilowatt hour to yield a $65,000,000 value of production. The estimate of sales for commerce, transportation, and services was derived from the Kenyan input/output model so that the same proportions of the total of the input/output for the sectors in Kenya were utilized for these sectors in Rhodesia [26]. In services and government sectors, a factor of 1.3 was used to estimate outlays relative to GDP. These crude estimates of outlays yielded the following estimates: traditional agriculture - $91.1 million, modern agriculture - $224.7 million, mining - $101.2 million, manufacturing - $757.2 million, building and construction - $115.8 million, utilities - $65 million, commerce - $469.5 million, transportation - $87 million, services - $198.9 million, government - $166.4 million, for a total of $2185.2 million. From these crude estimates of sales, the GDP in factor cost by industry of origin was deducted to get a preliminary estimate of inter-industry transfers. Table 51 of the August 1976 Digest of Statistics [12] provided the estimates of GDP in factor cost by industry of origin. The allocation of the inter-industry transfers used the following sources:

1. For the traditional sector, modern agri-culture, manufacturing, commerce, trans-portation, services and government, the Kenyan input/output distribution of inter-industry transfers was used [26].

2. Building and construction provided an analysis of the percentage of end use of output from Table 53 [12].

3. In the mining sector, it was estimated that coal constitutes about 12% of the mineral output of the country and it was assumed that this was used in the utili-ties and transportation and service sectors. It was also assumed that a considerable portion of the mining out-put would be re-processed through the manufacturing sector before it was exported. Page 310 and 311 of the Area Handbook for Southern Rhodesia provide preliminary estimates of the proportions of outputs by the type of product in 1965 [14]. From this it was estimated that 12% of the output was coal and thus domestically consumed rather than exported.

4. Utilities were estimated by report of
the percent of end use of output reported in Table 40 of the August 1976
Monthly Digest [12].

These preliminary adjustments of the inter-industry
transfers were checked against the National Income
statistics and then the matrix was subjected to a
balancing analysis developed by Robert Hess of the
University of Colorado Bureau of Economic Research.

Cards 200-390: private and government wages paid to
income classes. Table 50 of the August 1976 Monthly
Digest provides an estimate of total European and
African wages and by elimination, an estimate of
residual (or rental) income for Rhodesian households
[12]. Tables 16 and 17 also provide an estimate of
the dollar value of wages by sector for Africans and
Europeans. The distribution of income from wages was
estimated by also using Tables 14 and 15 which provide
estimates of the number of people employed in each
sector, both African and European. Thus a mean income per worker in each sector could be estimated
by dividing the wage totals by sector by race, by the
number of workers by race in each sector. The Whitson
Report provided further information upon which to
estimate the income per average African household in
various trades [28]. It was assumed that Europeans
are largely confined to the upper two categories,
C and D, of rural households and to the upper three
categories of urban households, G, H, and I. Subtracting total African employment from total African
household population, provides an estimate of the
number of households engaged in traditional agriculture as their principal means of economic support.

Cards 400-490: profit income to income classes
from processing sectors. Estimates of rental income
were made by subtracting wage income from GDP to
estimate the value added accruing to profits and other
residual income. Thus the sum of wages for all sectors,
government payments, depreciation and retained earnings subtracted from GDI, yields an estimate of
residual income (or rental income).

Cards 500 and 501: depreciation applicable to each
processing sector. Depreciation is estimated from
Table 53 of the August 1976 Monthly Digest of Statistics [12] which provides information on gross
fixed capital formation by sector. Removing government capital formation from the information

(approximately $25 million Rhodesian) and subtracting savings of approximately $60 million Rhodesian leaves a residual of about $125 million Rhodesian as private funds re-invested into the sectors according to the array of gross fixed capital formation.

Cards 510 and 511: indirect taxes paid by processing sectors. Using estimates from Table 50 of the August 1976 Monthly Digest of Statistics [12] of indirect taxes for 1971 of $97.9 million and the Central Government Budget Accounts (Table 57) on revenues, indirect taxes were allocated to sectors according to value added with some increase in the taxation of commerce to reflect a sales tax. (The commerce taxation was subtracted from manufacturing.)

Cards 520 and 521: subsidies to processing sectors. In 1971, subsidies reported in Table 50 of the August 1976 Monthly Digest of Statistics [12] netted out to zero.

Cards 530 and 531: interest paid to processing sectors. Interest paid to the services sector was estimated from Table 64 of the August 1976 Monthly Digest of Statistics [12] which reported advances to sectors. An interest rate of 6% was used to estimate the interest costs associated with these advances. In addition, on Table 24 agricultural loans in 1971 were estimated at $71.9 million.

Cards 540-544: imports by sector. Imports estimated by the London Economist Report [2] totaled $395 million Rhodesian. These were estimated to be approximately $150 million for intermediate imports (Cards 540 and 541), $150 million for capital imports (Cards 542 and 543) and $95 million for consumption reports (Cards 543 and 544). Allocation of the value of imports by sector and by type was based on KENSIM [26].

Cards 550 and 551: exports by sectors. Exports were estimated from the London Economist Report [2] to be $379 million Rhodesian. These are estimated to be $150 million agriculture, $169 million housing, $20 million manufacturing, $20 million commerce and $20 million transportation. The allocation was based on experience with the Kenyan simulation model [26].

Cards 560 and 561: stock changes by sector. Stock changes were reported on Table 57 of the August 1976 Digest of Statistics [12] to be $60.4 million in 1971.

Sector stock changes were estimated quite arbitrarily: refinement of this input would be useful.

Cards 570 and 571: investment by sector.

Cards 580 and 581: capital formation by sector. Fixed capital formation was estimated in Table 53 of the August 1976 Monthly Digest of Statistics [12] to be $227.8 million and the breakdown by sector was provided in the table. Capital formation is the investment in sectors that produces changes in the output of that sector. Whereas investment, as reported on cards 570-571 records the money spent in a particular sector. Thus, for example, building and construction looms large in the investment input but is relatively small in the capital formation input.

Cards 600 through 641: conversion matrix. The conversion matrix channels the output of the nine sectors through the four sectors of the economy from which the consumer can make direct purchases; traditional, utilities, commerce, and services. These conversion flows match the consumption matrix derived from the input/output estimates of value flows from these four sectors. Government consumption is estimated from Table 52 of the August 1976 Monthly Digest of Statistics [12].

Card 700: number of households in each income class. The number of households in each income class is estimated from Tables 1 and 2 of the August 1976 Monthly Digest [10] which report the number of African, European, Asian and other people in the nation and the urban estimates respectively. On page 5, the Whitson Report, "A Program for National Development," [28] provides estimates of African family incomes for the traditional agriculture sector, modern agriculture, mining, manufacturing and a combination of commerce, transportation and services, in contrast to domestic services and others.

Card 710: income per household, by income class. The income per household was initially estimated from the wage information discussed earlier and the employment information, together with the Whitson Report [28]. These early estimates were then adjusted to yield an income from wages and rents that is consistent with the National Income Accounts on Table 50 of the August 1976 Monthly Digest [12].

114

Card 720: taxes paid by income class. Total taxes by income class were estimated by subtracting the indirect taxes reported in Table 50 of the August 1976 Monthly Digest of Statistics [12] from the total of government revenues reported in Table 57. Allocation by income class is based on the KENSIM experience [26].

Card 730: savings by income class. Savings were estimated to be at 6% of personal income from wages plus rents and allocated by the authors' estimates to the upper income categories.

Card 740: allocation of consumer savings for investment in sectors. The application of consumer savings to sectors for investment were allocated in proportion to the total fixed capital formation in the private sector as reported in Table 53 of the August 1976 Monthly Digest [12].

Cards 800 through 850: consumption matrix. The consumption matrix allocates consumer demand by income class on the traditional sector, utilities, commerce, services, intermediate imports and duties on imports. Table 52 of the August 1976 Monthly Digest [12] reports traditional consumption to be $70.7 million. This is allocated to rural households by the author's estimates. Table 54, private consumption expenditures, was used to estimate total utilities consumption and the demand for utilities was allocated by income class according to the author's estimate. Similarly, Table 54 was utilized to generate estimates of the total demand for commerce and services. The total of durable and non-durable goods less the value of utilities provided an estimate of $410 million: this was allocated among income classes by the author's estimates. The duty on consumption imports was estimated at 10% of the value of the imports.

Cards 900 to 930: income transfers. Income transfers from middle income households to lower income households were estimated to be $7.2 million from Class F to Classes A and B, $31.5 million from Class G to Classes A, B, and C. No other income class transfers were estimated to be operating in Rhodesia at this time. These estimates are based on Kenyan experience [26].

115

Card 1000: government investment, deficit, loans, loan service. Government investment is estimated from several sources. Table 57 of the August 1976 Monthly Digest of Statistics [12] provides an estimate of government capital investment of $25 million, with the deficit in 1972-73 reported to be about $9.4 million. Loan service costs were the sum of central government loan services expenditures from Table 55 and local government expenditures from Table 56, totaling $726 million and interest costs of the central government reported in Table 57 of $27 million.

Card 1100: capacity utilization. Capacity utilization figures were authors' estimates and set relatively high because of the probable impact of the embargo forcing a high rate of utilization of the internal economy. This is consistent with the evidence of the high growth rate experienced by the economy.

Cards 1200 to 1290: employment matrix. Tables 14 and 15 of the August 1976 Monthly Digest [12] provide a basis for estimating the total African and European employment by sector. The European and colored employment were estimated to be largely confined to the upper income categories. This information, combined with the information on wages, provides a basis for authors' estimates of allocation of wage income by income class by sector.

Deck II - Difference Equation Inputs from 1972 Data

Cards 2000 and 2001: growth rate. The growth rate by sector was calculated for each sector from Table 51 of the August 1976 Monthly Digest [12].

Cards 2100 and 2101: capital capacity ratios. The capacity increase per dollar of capital investment is estimated by ratios of sector value added changes from Table 50 of the August 1976 Monthly Digest [12] and gross capital formation from Table 53.

Cards 2200 through 2261: matrix of changes in technical coefficients. The technical coefficients of output to capital were not utilized in this modeling exercise. The system is designed to reflect changes in the output of a sector relative to changes in input factor service cost.

Cards 2300 and 2301: price of imports. The price of imports was estimated to experience an average 4% increase in 1972, over 1971.

116

Cards 2310 and 2311: price of wages. The price of wages was estimated from Tables 14-17 of the August 1976 Monthly Digest of Statistics [12] to indicate the average wage changes for each sector, and for Africans and Europeans.

Cards 2320 and 2321: price of residualist income. The changes in value added, derived from Table 51 of the August 1976 Monthly Digest [12] relative to the changes in wages gave a basis for estimating growth in residualist income.

Cards 2330 and 2331: price of depreciation. The changes in retained earnings and depreciation were estimated from Table 50, National Income Accounts of the August 1976 Digest [12]. They were then adjusted by sector growth differentials from Table 51.

Cards 2340 and 2341: price of interest. Interest rates were estimated from Table 17 of the August 1976 Monthly Digest [12] to be constant from 1971 to 1972.

Cards 2350 and 2351: price of taxes. Tax rates for indirect taxes were estimated to have remained constant over the 1971-1972 period. This estimate is based on review of Tables 55 to 59, Government Finance, of the August 1976 Monthly Digest [12].

Cards 2360, 2361, and 2400: price impacts. These are estimates of the impact of price changes upon the sectors of the economy, and effects on consumers of changes in tax rates, savings, imports, and transfer payments. Estimates are based on the preceding price effects and the KENSIM experience [26].

Card 2500: population growth rate. The population growth rate of 3.4% and urbanization rate of 6% per year are estimated from Tables 2 and 3 of the August 1976 Monthly Digest [12].

Card 2510: emigration by income class. Estimates were made of the emigration by income class. This input is used to reflect scenarios of European departure from Rhodesia.

Deck III - The 1973, 1974, and 1975 Simulation Calibration and Test Data

Card 1: government debt and debt service. Government debt and service costs are estimated with

117

reference to Tables 55 and 56 of the August 1976
Monthly Digest [12].

Card 2: government consumption, capital formation
and subsidies. Table 52 of the August 1976 Monthly
Digest [12] estimates government consumption, capital
formation, and subsidies.

Card 3: government investment. Government investment estimates by sector come from two tables in the
August 1976 Monthly Digest [12]: Table 52 provides
the total and the breakdown is indicated on Table 53.

Card 4: private foreign investment. Net inflow on
current and capital accounts is estimated from Table
49 of the August 1976 Monthly Digest [12].

Cards 10 and 11: building/construction and services
capital effect. These are the proportions of capital
investment expended through the building/construction
and services sectors. These estimates are based on
the Kenyan experience [26].

Card 15: exports. Exports were estimated from the
same source used in the base deck.

Card 16: stock changes. Stock changes were derived
from Table 52 of the August 1976 Monthly Digest [12]
with authors' allocation estimates.

Card 50: capital capacity ratios. These ratios are
based on figures from the August 1976 Monthly Digest
[12]. The ratio of capital investment needed to
expand capacity is estimated from the ratio of capital
investment by sector (Table 53) and value added by
sector (Table 51).

In order to reflect the declining efficiency of the
system under new and inexperienced managers, these
coefficients were later raised to reflect mild and
severe transitional problems.

Cards 51 through 57: changes in technical coefficients. Technical coefficient responses were
not utilized in this simulation.

Card 20: weather factor. This card reflects changes
in output of traditional and modern agriculture to
reflect weather and other similar exogenous changes.
This variable was used to represent management
efficiency declines in modern agriculture.

Cards 60 through 67: price effects. These cards
reflect estimates of price and factor service costs
and are identical to Cards 2300 to 2400 in Deck II.

Card 70: population growth and urbanization. Population and urbanization estimates were made as on
Card 2500 in Deck II. In later years, the rate of
urban drift is varied to reflect the easing of con-
trols on African domicile location.

Card 80: emigration rate. The emigration of
Europeans; same as card 2510 of Deck II.

Card 90: agricultural demand shift factor. This
card allows transfer of effective demand between
modern agriculture and traditional agriculture.

Deck IV - 1976-1985 Policy Data

The role within the model of these cards is identical
to the cards in Deck II. The data sources here are
estimates of the policies set by the external environment or the government.

Flow Chart of ZIMSIM

Start ZIMSIM
↓
Balance Base Period Data
↓
Calculate Coefficients
↓
Input Second Period Growth Rates
↓
Calculate Base Period Investments
↓
Start Simulation by Period
(reading in each period's data as required)
↓
Calculate Prices
↓
Calculate Inflation Rates
↓
Calculate Money Flows from Productive Sectors to
Households
↓
Income Distribution Algorithm
↓
Population Outmigration
↓
Employment by Industry and Income Class
↓
Calculate Unconstrained Demand
↓
Calculate Constrained Demand
(balance to Imports)
↓
Government Investment and Taxes
↓
Capital Formation
↓
Construction Effect
↓
Calculate Exports
↓
Calculate Investments
↓
Calculate Sector Output Needed to Meet Demand
↓
Calculate Productive Capacity and Imports
↓
Repeat for Remaining Periods
↓
Calculate Growth Rates
↓
Stop ZIMSIM

Equations of ZIMSIM

The following 50 model equations are translated into computer code as subsequently presented here. The equations represent the processing of inputs from a neo-Keynesian point of view.

Conventions

The subscripts i,j will be used to denote productive or sales sectors and the subscripts k,l to denote income classes. There are 10 sectors and 9 income classes. The letter n denotes the model year.

Endogenous Variables - two dimensional array

$A_{ij}(n)$ input/output matrix coefficient giving the input from sector i to sector j divided by the gross output of sector j (in year n). See equation 2.

CD_{kj} consumption propensity of income class k for the output of sales sector j ($j=1,4$)

EM_{ki} no. of jobs provided in income class k per unit of output from sector i

JB_{ki} no. of jobs provided in income class k by sector i

RN_{ki} rental income to class k per unit of output from sector i

TF_{kl} income transfer from class l to class k

WG_{ki} government wage income to class k per unit of output from sector i

WP_{ki} private wage income to class k per unit of output from sector i

Endogenous Variables - one dimensional array

cc_i capacity of sector i

121

cf_i capital formation in sector i

$ch_k(n)$ thousands of households moving from class k to class (k+1) in year n to year (n+1)

co_i consumption imports to sector i

cr_i capital formation in sector i

ct_i demand on sector i created by construction effect of capital investment

de_i depreciation in sector i per unit of gross output

dep_i depreciation in sector i

dp_i consumer demand for the output of sector i

ds_j consumer demand for the output of sales sector j (j=1,4)

fd_i final demand on sector i

go_i gross output of sector i

$gold_i(n)$ gross output of sector i in year n in year (n+1) prices

$gr_i(n)$ growth rate of sector i from year (n-1) to year n

hi_k consumption propensity in income class k for direct imports

hn_k thousands of households in income class k

hs_k savings propensity in class k

ht_k taxation propensity in class k

hy_k income/household in class k

icm_k total income in class k

im_i intermediate imports to sector i per unit of gross output

$inc_k(n)$ ratio of class k income in year (n+1) over year n

it_i interest payments by sector i per unit of gross output

nw_k thousands of households without wage employment in class k

$p_i(n)$ price inflation ratio for the output of sector i from year n to year (n+1)

$pc_j(n)$ price inflation ratio to consumers of the output of sales sector j from year n to year (n+1)

phn_k provisional value for thousands of households in class k

q_i measure of cost inflation for sector i inputs

rc_i capital formation less capital imports for sector i

re_i rent paid by sector i

ren_k total rental income to class k

sv_i total consumer savings allocated to sector i

ti_k total income to class k

tw_k thousands of households with wage employment in class k

tx_i indirect tax on sector i per unit of gross output

ugo_i uncorrected gross output of sector i

wag_k total wage income to class k

wg_i wages paid by sector i

wp_i weighted price change of productive sector i goods including consumption imports

Endogenous Variables - single variables

capimd   duty on capital imports

capimp	value of capital imports
condut	duty on direct consumer imports
conimp	value of direct consumer imports
consav	value of consumer savings
contax	total consumer taxes
def	government deficit
govexp	total government expenditure
govinc	total government income
poprur	rural population growth rate
ra	adjustment factor for rural population numbers
rurpop	total rural population
totgr(n)	overall economic growth rate from year (n-1) to year n
totimd	duty on intermediate imports
totitx	total indirect taxation
ua	adjustment factor for urban population numbers
urbpop	total urban population

Exogenous Variables - two dimensional arrays

P_{im}	price inflation rate in sector i for imports, wages, rents, depreciation, interest, and taxes (m=1, 6, respectively).
TC_{im}	the effect of R$10 million of investment in sector i on technical coefficients for inputs, imports, wages, rents, depreciation, interest, and taxes (m=1, 7, respectively. e.g. if $TC_{i2} = 0.99$, this implies that R$10 million of investment in sector i will reduce by 1 percent the jobs/unit of output ratio in the total sector.

Exogenous Variables - one dimensional arrays

bc_i — proportion of capital investment in sector i resulting in a demand on the Building and Construction sector

$caprat_i$ — capital/capacity ratio for sector i

cn_i — constraint on demand

ex_i — sector i exports

f_i — population migration factor. $1-f_i$ of the income group migrates from the country

gv_i — government investment in sector i

prc_m — price inflation rates for consumer taxes, savings, direct imports, transfers, and class E negative savings (m=1, 5, respectively)

pv_i — private investment in sector i

$serv_i$ — proportion of capital investment in sector i resulting in a demand on the Services sector

st_i — sector i stock change

Exogenous Variables - single elements

ag — agricultural weather variable

govcon — government consumption expenditure

govl — loans to government

govls — government loan service payments

poptot — overall population growth rate

popurb — urban population growth rate

subs — subsidies to modern agriculture

Model Constants

CV_{ij} — proportion of the demand for sales sector j (j=1,4) which results in a demand on productive sector i

a_k a set of constants approximately inversely proportional to the difference $hy_{(k+1)} - hy_k$

ci_i proportion of capital imports to capital investment in sector i

cs_i proportion of consumer savings allocated to sector i for investment

dt_k rate of duty on consumer imports to class k

id_i rate of duty on capital imports to sector i

itd_i rate of duty on intermediate imports to sector i

Model Equations

Base year data and second year data are used to calculate initial values for the variables. Model years are then generated using model equations listed below in Dynamic Model Equations 3-50.

NOTE   The following notation is used:

1. $\underline{x}(n)$ will be taken to mean the one dimensional array

$$\begin{bmatrix} x_1(n) \\ \cdot \\ \cdot \\ x_r(n) \end{bmatrix}$$ where the number of elements r

is given by the variable definitions earlier in this chapter.

2. X' denotes the transpose of the one dimensional array X so that $\underline{x}'(n) = (x_1[n], \ldots, x_r[n])$.

Base Year Balance Equations - (the Accounting Balance)

Equation 1 is the first of the balance checks. It represents total income. For each income class $k(k=1,9)$, the total income to that class can be

126

expressed in three ways: (1) as sum of the products
of the number of households in the classes times the
income per household in each class; (2) as the sum
of wages, rents, and transfer income to the classes;
(3) as the sum of the total expenditures of the
classes on taxes, savings, direct imports, and internal consumption.

$$\text{icm}_k(1) = \text{hn}_k(1) \cdot \text{hy}_k(1)$$

$$= \text{wag}_k(1) + \text{ren}_k(1) + \sum_{\ell=1}^{9} \text{TF}_{k\ell}(1) \qquad (1)$$

$$= [\text{ht}_k(1) + \text{hs}_k(1) + \text{hi}_k(1) \sum_{J=1}^{4} \text{CD}_{jk}(1)]$$

Equation 2 provides a balance check for the
gross output of each of the productive sectors
i(i=1,10). The total value of inputs to the sector,
including rental payments, should equal the total
value of goods produced by the sector. Thus for a
given sector i, the sum of inputs from productive
sectors, intermediate imports, wages, rents, depreciation, interest, and indirect taxes, less subsidies, should equal the sum of private consumption,
government consumption, intermediate use by productive sectors, exports, the construction effect
demand from investment, and stock change.

$$\text{go}_i(1) = \text{go}_i(1) \; [\sum_{J=1}^{10} A_{ji}(1) + \text{im}_i(1) + \text{it}_i(1)$$

$$+ \text{tx}_i(1)] + \text{wg}_i(1) + \text{re}_i(1)$$

$$+ \text{dep}_i(1) \; [- \text{subs for i=2}]$$

$$= \text{dp}_i(1) \; [+ \text{govcon for l=10}] + \sum_{J=1}^{10} A_{ij}(1) \; \text{go}_j(1)$$

$$+ \text{ex}_i(1) + \text{ct}_i(1) + \text{st}_i(1) \qquad (2)$$

Dynamic Model - equations 3-50

This section contains the remainder of the
model equations.

Consumption demands in each income class draw
upon the four sales sectors by way of equation 3.
Equation 4 describes how the demands on the four

sales sectors create demand on the ten productive
sectors.

$$ds(n) = h(n) \cdot CD(n) \tag{3}$$

$$dp_i(n) = \sum_{j=1}^{4} CV_{ij} \cdot ds_j(n) \, (i \neq 9) \tag{4}$$

$$dp_9(n) = govcon$$

Equation 5 describes the manner in which demand
is constrained due to population flight.

$$dp_i(n) = dp_i(n) \cdot (1-cn_i)$$

$$dp_4(n) = dp_4(n) + \sum_{i=1}^{10} dp_i(n) \cdot (1-cn_i) \tag{5}$$

Consumer taxes, savings and demand for consumption imports are calculated based on household
incomes and fractional constants as described in
equations 6, 7, and 8 respectively. Duty on consumer
imports is calculated in equation 9.

$$contax(n) = h(n) \cdot ht(n) \tag{6}$$

$$consav(n) = h(n) \cdot hs(n) \tag{7}$$

$$conimp(n) = h(n) \cdot hi(n) \tag{8}$$

$$condut(n) = h(n) \cdot d'(n) \tag{9}$$

Government income in equation 10 is the sum of
indirect taxes, consumer taxes, intermediate import
duties, capital import duties, duties on consumer
imports and of loans to government.

$$
\begin{aligned}
govinc(n) = \; & totitx(n) + contax(n) \\
& + totimd(n) + capimd(n-1) \\
& + condut(n) + govl(n) \tag{10}
\end{aligned}
$$

Capital formation, as contributed by government is equation 11.

$$govcap(n) = \sum_{i=1}^{10} gv_i(n) \tag{11}$$

Government expenditures, equation 12, are the sum of government consumption, capital formation, subsidies, and loan repayment. This is an exogenous policy estimated for each year. Deficit, equation 13, is the difference between expenditures and income.

$$govexp(n) = govcon(n) + govcap(n) \quad (12)$$
$$+ subs(n) + govls(n)$$

$$def(n) = govexp(n) - govinc(n) \quad (13)$$

Depreciation, equation 14, is a predefined proportion of previous period's gross output.

$$\underline{dep}(n) = \underline{gold}'(n-1) \cdot \underline{de}(n-1) \quad (14)$$

Savings, equation 15, is the total savings for the period distributed according to the characteristic savings rate.

$$\underline{sv}(n) = consav(n) \cdot \underline{cs} \quad (15)$$

Capital formation is the sum of government investment, foreign private investment, depreciation, and invested savings (equation 16).

$$\underline{cf}(n) = \underline{gv}(n) + \underline{pv}(n) + \underline{dep}(n) + \underline{sv}(n) \quad (16)$$

Equation 17 subtracts capital imports from total capital formation.

$$rc_i(n) = cf_i(n) \ (1-ci_i) \ (i=1,9) \quad (17)$$

Equation 18 describes the capital construction effect.

$$ct_i(n) = rc_i(n) \ [1-bc_i(n) - serv_i(n)]$$
$$(i \neq 4,8)$$

$$ct_4(n) = rc_4(n) \ [1-bc_4(n) - serv_4(n)]$$
$$+ \sum_{i=1}^{9} rc_i(n) \cdot bc_i(n) \quad (18)$$

$$ct_8(n) = rc_8(n) \ [1-bc_8(n) - serv_8(n)]$$
$$+ \sum_{i=1}^{9} rc_i(n) \cdot serv_i(n)$$

Final demand, equation 19, is described by the sum of consumer demand, construction effects, exports, and stock changes.

$$\underline{fd}(n) = \underline{dp}(n) + \underline{ct}(n) + \underline{ex}(n) + \underline{st}(n) \qquad (19)$$

Capital imports, equation 20, is determined by the level of capital investment and by capital imports needed.

$$capimp(n) = \underline{cf}'(n) \cdot \underline{ci} \qquad (20)$$

Duty on capital imports, equation 21, is determined by the duty rate previously established.

$$capimd(n) = \sum_{i=1}^{9} cf_i(n) \cdot ci_i \cdot id_i \qquad (21)$$

Equation 22 takes into account capital investment's ability to increase sector capacities.

$$cc_i(n) = cc_i(n-1) \cdot wp_i(n-1) + \frac{cf_i(n) \, [1-de_i(n)]}{caprat_i(n)}$$

$$(22)$$

In equation 23 the technical coefficients are reached.

$$\underline{cr}(n) = \frac{1}{10,000} \cdot \underline{cf}(n) \qquad (23)$$

Equations 24 describe the way the model's technical coefficients can be updated.

Define $\quad F_{im}(n) = 1 - cr_i(n) + cr_i(n) \cdot TC_{im}$

$$A_{ij}(n) = A_{ij}^p(n-1) \cdot F_{j7}$$

$$WP_{ki}(n) = WP_{ki}^p(n-1) \cdot F_{i2}$$

$$WG_{ki}(n) = WG_{ki}^p(n-1) \cdot F_{i2} \qquad (24)$$

$$EM_{ki}(n) = EM_{ki}^p(n-1) \cdot F_{i2}$$

$$RN_{ki}(n) = RN_{ki}^p(n-1) \cdot F_{i3}$$

$$de_i(n) = de_i^p(n-1) \cdot F_{i4}$$

$$im_i(n) = im_i^p(n-1) \cdot F_{i1}$$

130

$$it_i(n) = it_i^p(n-1) \cdot F_{i5} \qquad \text{(24 cont)}$$

$$tx_i(n) = tx_i^p(n-1) \cdot F_{i6}$$

(The superscript p indicates that the coefficients for the year n-1 have been updated to year n prices.)

Equation 25 solves the matrix equation, which is a function of final demand and of sector I/O, for gross output.

$$\underline{ugo}(n) = [I - A(n)]^{-1} \cdot \underline{fd}(n) \qquad (25)$$

Equation 26 is a model representation of importing that proportion of demand that can not be satisfied domestically.

$$co_i(n) = \max [0, \, ugo_i(n) - cc_i(n)] \qquad (26)$$

Equation 27 corrects provisional gross output by imports to final output.

$$\underline{go}(n) = \underline{ugo}(n) - \underline{co}(n) \qquad (27)$$

Equation 28 describes sector growths.

$$gr_i(n) = \frac{go_i(n)}{gold_i(n-1)} \qquad (28)$$

Equation 29 is the entire economic's growth rate.

$$totgr(n) = \frac{\sum_{i=1}^{10} go_i(n)}{\sum_{j=1}^{10} gold_i(n-1)} \qquad (29)$$

Equations 30, 31, and 32 are the model price equations. Equation 30 defines cost inflation, equation 31 determines intermediate consumption prices, and equation 32 changes gross output to current price levels.

$$q_i(n) = \underline{inp}(i,n) \cdot \underline{p}_i' \qquad (30)$$

$$\underline{p}(n) = (I - A'(n))^{-1} \cdot \underline{q}(n) \qquad (31)$$

$$gold_i(n) = go_i(n) \cdot p_i(n) \qquad (32)$$

131

Equation 33 is the weighted price of goods for each sector.

$$wp_i(n) = p_i(n) \cdot \left[1 + \frac{co_i(n) \, (pim_i(n) - 1)}{ugo_i(n)} \right]$$

(33)

Equation 34 is the price of goods for the sales sectors.

$$pc_j(n) = \frac{\sum\limits_{i=1}^{10} wp_i(n) \cdot CV_{ij}}{\sum\limits_{i=1}^{10} CV_{ij}}$$

(34)

Equation 35 represents the inflation factors of the sectors.

$$inf_k(n) = ht_k(n) \cdot prc_1(n) + hs_k(n) \cdot prc_2(n)$$

$$+ hi_k(n) \cdot prc_3(n) + \sum\limits_{i=1}^{4} CD_{kj}(n) \cdot pc_j(n)$$

(35)

Price increases of transfers between income groups is expressed in equation 36.

$$TF(n+1) = prc_4(n) \, TF(n)$$

(36)

Equation 37 calculates the incomes necessary for each class to sustain a real income.

$$hy_k(n+1) = hy_k(n) \cdot inf_k(n)$$

$$ht_k(n+1) = \frac{ht_k(n) \cdot prc_1(n)}{inf_k(n)}$$

$$hs_k(n+1) = \frac{hs_k(n) \cdot prc_2(n)}{inf_k(n)}$$

$$hi_k(n+1) = \frac{hi_k(n) \cdot prc_3(n)}{inf_k(n)}$$

$$CD_{kj}(n+1) = \frac{CD_{kj}(n) \cdot pc_j(n)}{inf_k(n)}$$

(37)

132

Price adjustments to factor inputs are calculated in equation 38.

$$A_{ij}{}^P(n) = A_{ij}(n) \cdot wp_i(n)/wp_j(n)$$

$$WP_{ki}{}^P(n) = WP_{ki}(n) \cdot P_{i2}(n)/wp_i(n)$$

$$WG_{ki}{}^P(n) = WG_{ki}(n) \cdot P_{i2}(n)/wp_i(n)$$

$$EM_{ki}{}^P(n) = EM_{ki}(n)/wp_i(n) \qquad (38)$$

$$RN_{ki}{}^P(n) = RN_{ki}(n) \cdot P_{i3}(n)/wp_i(n)$$

$$de_i{}^P(n) = de_i(n) \cdot P_{i4}(n)/wp_i(n)$$

$$im^P{}_i(n) = im_i(n) \cdot P_{i1}(n)/wp_i(n)$$

$$it_i{}^P(n) = it_i(n) \cdot P_{i5}(n)/wp_i(n)$$

Payments to factors are described in 39 and 40.

$$tx^P{}_i(n) = tx_i(n) \cdot P_{i6}(n)/wp_i(n)$$

$$go^P{}_i(n) = go_i(n) \cdot wp_i(n)$$

$$\underline{wag}(n+1) = (WP^P(n) + WG^P(n)) \cdot \underline{go}^P(n)$$

$$\underline{ren}(n+1) = RN^P(n) \cdot \underline{go}^P(n) \qquad (39)$$

$$totitx(n+1) = \underline{go}^{P'}(n) \cdot \underline{tx}^P(n)$$

$$totimp(n+1) = \underline{go}^{P'}(n) \cdot \underline{im}^P(n) \qquad (40)$$

$$totimd(n+1) = \sum_{i=1}^{9} go^P{}_i(n) \cdot im_i{}^P(n) \cdot itd_i$$

Rural and urban population levels are calculated in equations 41 and 42.

$$rurpop(n) = \sum_{k=1}^{4} hn_k(n)$$

$$\qquad (41)$$

$$urbpop(n) = \sum_{k=5}^{9} hn_k(n)$$

$$\text{urbpop}(n+1) = \text{urbpop}(n) \cdot \text{popurb}(n)$$

$$\text{rurpop}(n+1) = [\text{rurpop}(n) + \text{urbpop}(n)]$$

$$\text{poptot}(n) - \text{urbpop}(n+1)$$

$$\text{poprur}(n+1) = \text{rurpop}(n+1)/\text{rurpop}(n)$$

$$(42)$$

Equations 43 through 48 describe the iterative income distribution algorithm, the underlying constraint of which is a constant real income.

$$\text{icm}_k(n+1) = \text{wag}_k(n+1) + \text{ren}_k(n+1)$$

$$+ \sum_{l=1}^{9} \text{TF}_{kl}(n+1) \qquad (43)$$

$$\text{inc}_k(n) = \text{icm}_k(n+1)/\text{icm}_k(n)$$

$$\text{ch}_k(n) = \text{hn}_k(n) \cdot a_k \cdot (\text{inc}_k(n)$$

$$- \text{inf}_k(n)) \quad (k \neq 4,9) \qquad (44)$$

subject to

$$-0.3 \times \text{hn}_{k+1}(n) \leq \text{ck}_k(n)$$

$$\leq 0.3 \times \text{hn}_{k+1}(n) \quad (k=3,8)$$

$$\text{phn}_1(n+1) = \text{hn}_1(n) - d_1(n) + \text{rurpop}(n) [\text{poprur}(n)-1]$$

$$\text{hn}_k(n+1) = \text{hn}_k(n) + d_{k-1}(n) - {}_k(n) \quad (k=2,3,6,7,8)$$

$$\text{phn}_5(n+1) = \text{hn}_5(n) - d_5(n) + \text{urbpop}(n) [\text{popurb}(n)-1]$$

$$\text{phn}_k(n+1) = \text{hn}_k(n) + d_{k-1}(n) \quad (k=4,9) \qquad (45)$$

$$\sum_{k=1,4} phn_k(n+1)\,hy_k(n+1) + \sum_{k=2,3} hn_k(n+1) \cdot$$

$$ra(n) = \frac{hy_k(n+1) - \sum_{i=1}^{4} icm_k(n+1)}{hy_4(n+1) - hy_1(n1+)} \qquad (46)$$

$$\sum_{k=5,9} phn_k(n+1) \cdot hy_k(n+1) - \sum_{k=6}^{8} hn_k(n+1) \cdot$$

$$ua(n) = \frac{hy_k(n+1) - \sum_{k=5}^{9} icm_k(n+1)}{hy_9(n+1) - hy_5(n+1)} \qquad (47)$$

$$hn_1(n+1) = phn_1(n+1) + ra(n)$$

$$hn_4(n+1) = phn_4(n+1) - ra(n)$$

$$hn_5(n+1) = phn_5(n+1) + ua(n) \qquad (48)$$

$$hn_9(n+1) = phn_9(n+1) - ua(n)$$

Equation 49 describes reduction in household members as a result of population flight.

$$hn_i(n) = hn_i(n) \cdot fi \qquad (49)$$

Equations 50 describe the method of calculating the number of jobs in each sector/household.

$$JB_{ki}(n+1) = EM_{ki}^{p}(n) \cdot go_i^{p}(n)$$

$$tw_k(n+1) = \sum_{i=1}^{9} JB_{ki}(n+1) \qquad (50)$$

$$nw_k(n+1) = hn_k(n+1) - tw_k(n+1)$$

The manner in which these equations are used can be seen in the computer code in the final section of this Appendix.

Code of ZIMSIM

```
      PROGRAM ZIMSIM(INPUT,OUTPUT,TAPE1=INPUT,TAPE2=OUTPUT)

C  THIS IS THE MASTER CALLING ROUTINE FOR THE PROGRAM ZIMSIM. ZIMSIM IS
C  THE SIMULATION OF THE RHODESIAN (ZIMBABWE) ECONOMY.
C
C  ZIMSIM IS BUILT ON THE BASIS OF THE KENYAN MODEL ORIGINALLY BY C.SLATER
C  AND G. WALSHAM
C  AUTHOR L. POOK DECEMBER 12, 1976
C
C  SET THE READ AND WRITE CHANNEL NUMBERS                                   021
      DIMENSION ARRAY(9),SECTOR(10),GO(10),GROW(10)
      DIMENSION RIO(10,10),WP(9,10),WG(9,10),RN(9,10)
      DIMENSION DEPR(10),RITX(10), RINT(10), RIMP(10), RIMT(10)
      DIMENSION CCNV(10,5), HSDN(9), TAXS(9), SAVG(9)
      DIMENSION CONS(10,4), TRAF(9,4), RIMD(9), RDUT(9)
      DIMENSION RIMC(10), CAPF(10), COSV(10), CAPUT(10)
      DIMENSION PIMP(10), PWAG(10), PREN(10), PDEP(10), PINT(10)
      DIMENSION PTAX(10), CAPAC(10)
      DIMENSION CONST(10), FD(10), WAGES(9), RENTS(9), FACINF(9),YOLD(9)
      DIMENSION CONSIM(10), CONDEM(10), PRICE(10), SUBS(10), TOTCOV(9)
      DIMENSION EMPLOY(9,10)
      DIMENSION BASEGO(10)
      DIMENSION GOLD(10)
      DIMENSION REXP(10), RINV(10), STOC(10)
      COMMON/BLOCK1/ARRAY,SECTOR,GO,NYEAR,NI,NO,NBASE
      COMMON/CLOCK2/RIO,WP,WG,RN,DEPR,RITX,RINT,RIMP,RIMT               017
      COMMON/BLOCK3/CONV,HSDN,YHSD,TAXS,SAVG,CONS,TRAF,RIMD,RDUT        018
      COMMON/BLOCK4/RIMC,CAPF,COSV,CAPUT
      COMMON/BLOCK5/PIMP,PWAG,PREN,PDEP,PINT,PTAX
      NI=1                                                             020
      NO=2                                                             022
C  HEADERS READS NAMES OF CONSUMER CLASSES AND OF PRODUCTIVE SECTORS
C  WITH BASEYEAR AND TIME HORIZON FOR FORECASTING
      CALL HEADERS(NPER,NEND)
C  BASEYR READS IN BASE YEAR DATA
      CALL BASEYR(SUBS,EMPLOY,STOC,REXP,RINV)
C  BANNER WRITES GENERAL PROGRAM ID.S
      CALL BANNER(NPER)
C  BALANCE MAKES BALANCE CHECKS ON THE BASE YEAR DATA
      CALL BALANCE(TOTCOV,SUBS,STOC,REXP,RINV)
C  COEFF CONVERTS THE BASE PERIOD I/O DATA AND HOUSEHOLD CONSUMPTION DATA    035
C  INTO SCALED COEFFICIENTS FOR USE IN LATER YEARS                          036
```

137

```
      CALL COEFF(TOTCOV,CAPAC,EMPLOY)                                    037
C READ IN 1971-2 GROWTH RATES IN GROSS QUANTITY OUTPUT OF 10 SECTORS
      CALL READV4(GROW)                                                 041
C CALCULATE 1972. GROSS OUTPUTS
      DO 10 I=1,10                                                      043
      BASEGO(I)=GO(I)                                                   044
      GO(I)=GO(I)*GROW(I)                                               045
      GOLD(I)=GO(I)                                                     046
      CONSIM(I)=0                                                       047
   10 CONTINUE                                                          048
      NYEAR=1972                                                        049
C INVEST MAKES AMENDMENTS TO TECHNICAL COEFFICIENTS AND CAPACITY DUE TO
C CAPITAL INVESTMENT
      CALL INVEST(CAPAC,CAPIMD,EMPLOY)                                  050
C NOW THE PROGRAM ENTERS THE MAIN DO-LOOP WHICH IS REPEATED ONCE FOR    051
C EACH SIMULATED YEAR-IT CONSISTS OF A SERIES OF SUBROUTINE CALLS       052
      NLAST=NEND+1                                                      053
      DO 100 IPER=1,NPER                                                054
C PRICEC READS IN PRICE CHANGES IN IMPORTS,WAGES,RENTS,DEPRECIATION,
C INTEREST AND TAXES.IT THEN CALCULATES THE 10 SECTOR NEW OUTPUT PRICES
      CALL PRICEC(PRICE,CAPAC,GOLD)                                     058
C INFLATION CALCULATES THE NEW PRICES OF THE 4 DIRECT CONSUMPTION SECTOR 060
C OUTPUTS AND THUS CALCULATES THE NEW INCOME/HOUSEHOLD FOR GROUPS A-I   061
C TAKING PRICE INFLATION INTO ACCOUNT                                   062
      CALL INFLAT(FACINF,YOLD,CONSIM,PRICE)                             063
C PAYMENTS CALCULATES WAGES,RENTS,TAXES PAYED BY THE 10 SECTORS OF THE
C ECONOMY.ALSO AMENDS THE TECH CCEFFS TO TAKE ACCOUNT OF PRICE CHANGE   066
      CALL PAYMNT(WAGES,RENTS,PRICE,TOTITX,TOTIMD,EMPLOY)
C REDISTRIBUTE USES DATA ON POPULATION INCREASE,MIGRATION AND INCOME    068
C TO ALLOCATE THE POPULATION AMONGST INCOME CLASSES                     069
      CALL REDIS(WAGES,RENTS,FACINF,YOLD)
C CONSTRAIN POPULATION NUMBERS DUE TO WHITE MIGRATION
      CALL BOATS                                                        071
C JOBS CALCULATES DETAILS OF WAGE EMPLOYMENT IN EACH INCOME CLASS
      CALL JOBS(EMPLOY)                                                 073
      NYEAR=NYEAR+1
      IF(NYEAR.EQ.NLAST)GO TO 110                                       075
      WRITE(NO,20)NYEAR                                                 076
   20 FORMAT(15H1START OF YEAR ,I4//)                                   077
C DEMAND CALCULATES TOTAL DEMAND FOR THE 4 DIRECT CONSUMPTION SECTORS
C AND CONVERTS THIS TO 10 SECTOR DEMAND.IT ALSO COMPUTES TOTAL CONSUMER
C TAXES,SAVINGS AND DIRECT IMPORTS                                      079
```

138

```
      CALL DEMAND(CONDEM,CONDUT,CONSAV,CONTAX)                              080
C GOVERNMENT COMPUTES GOVERNMENT INCOME,EXPENDITURE AND DEFICIT IT ALSO     081
C CALCULATES FINAL DEMAND ON THE GOVERNMENT SECTOR                         082
      CALL GOVERN(CONDEM,SUBS,CAPIMD,TOTITX,TOTIMD,CONDUT,CONTAX)        08
C CAPFORM CALCULATES CAPITAL FORMATION AS THE SUM OF CONSUMER SAVINGS,      084
C BUSINESS SAVINGS,GOVERNMENT CAPITAL EXPENDITURE AND PRIVATE CAPITAL       085
C IMPORTS                                                                   086
      CALL CAPFORM(CONSAV)
C CONSTEFF DETERMINES THE DEMAND ON THE 10 SECTORS GENERATED BY THE         089
C CONSTRUCTION EFFECT OF CAPITAL INVESTMENT
      CALL CONSTEF(CONST)
C EXPORT READS IN EXPORT AND STOCK CHANGE FIGURES AND COMPUTES FINAL        091
C DEMAND=CONSUMER DEMAND+GOV CONS+CONST EFFECT+EXPORTS+STOCK CHANGE         092
      CALL EXPORT(CONST,FD,CONDEM,SUBS)                                     093
C INVEST MAKES AMENDMENTS TO TECHNICAL COEFFICIENTS AND CAPACITY DUE TO     094
C CAPITAL INVESTMENT                                                        095
      CALL INVEST(CAPAC,CAPIMD,EMPLOY)                                      096
C PROD USES I/O ANALYSIS AND FINAL DEMAND DATA TO GENERATE THE GROSS        097
C OUTPUT OF THE 10 PRODUCTIVE SECTORS
      CALL PROD(FD,RIO)
C CAPACITY CHECKS IF THE PROVISIONAL GROSS OUTPUT OF EACH SECTOR IS         099
C WITHIN THE CAPACITY CONSTRAINT.IF NOT,THE BALANCE IS IMPORTED.            100
C IN THE CASE OF MODERN AGRICULTURE,A WEATHER FACTOR IS ALSO CONSIDERED     101
      CALL CAPCTY(CONSIM,CAPAC,GROW,GOLD)                                   102
C THIS COMPLETES THE MAIN DO-LOOP AND THE PROGRAM RETURNS TO THE START   103
C OF THE LOOP FOR ANOTHER YEAR UNLESS THE RUN IS COMPLETE IN WHICH CASE     104
C THE PROGRAM STOPS                                                         105
  100 CONTINUE                                                              106
C AT THE END OF THE RUN THE OVERALL GROWTH RATE IS CALCULATED              107
  110 CALL RATE(BASEGO,GROW,NEND)                                           108
      STOP
      END

      SUBROUTINE HEADERS(NPER,NEND)

C
C HEADERS READS NAMES OF CONSUMER CLASSES AND OF PRODUCTIVE SECTORS
C WITH BASE YEAR AND TIME HORIZON FOR FORECASTING
C
      DIMENSION ARRAY(9),SECTOR(10),GO(10),GROW(10)
      DIMENSION VERSN(2)
      COMMON/BLOCK1/ARRAY,SECTOR,GO,NYEAR,NI,NO,NBASE
      READ(NI,5)VERSN
```

```
5       FORMAT(2A4)
        WRITE(NO,6) VERSN
6       FORMAT(1H1,1X,8HVERSION ,2A4)
        READ(NI,1)ARRAY
1       FORMAT(9A1)
        READ(NI,2) SECTOR
2       FORMAT(10A6)
C READ BASE YEAR VALUE
        READ(NI,3) NYEAR
3       FORMAT(10X,I4)
        NBASE=NYEAR
C READ THE NUMBER OF YEARS (PERIODS) THE PROGRAM IS TO RUN
        READ(NI,4) NPER,NEND
4       FORMAT(16X,I2,12X,I4)
        RETURN
        END

        SUBROUTINE BASEYR(SUBS,EMPLOY,STOC,REXP,RINV,GSURPL,
C THIS SUBROUTINE READS IN THE BASE PERIOD DATA AND MAKES BALANCE CHECKS    124
        DIMENSION ARRAY(9),SECTOR(10),GO(10),GROW(10)
        DIMENSION RIO(10,10), WP(9,10), WG(9,10), RN(9,10)
        DIMENSION DEPR(10), RITX(10), RINT(10), RIMP(10), RIMT(10)
        DIMENSION CONV(10,5), HSDN(9), YHSD(9), TAXS(9), SAVG(9)
        DIMENSION CONS(10,4), TRAF(9,4), RIMD(9), RDUT(9)
        DIMENSION RIMC(10), CAPF(10), COSV(10), CAPUT(10)
        DIMENSION PIMP(10), PWAG(10), PREN(10), PDEP(10), PINT(10)
        DIMENSION PTAX(10), CAPAC(10)
        DIMENSION CONST(10), FD(10), WAGES(9), RENTS(9), FACINF(9),YOLD(9)
        DIMENSION CONSIM(10), CONDEM(10), PRICE(10), SUBS(10), TOTCOV(9)
        DIMENSION EMPLOY(9,10)
        DIMENSION FACTR(10)
        DIMENSION DUMMY(10)
        COMMON/BLOCK1/ARRAY,SECTOR,GO,NYEAR,NI,NO,NBASE
        COMMON/BLOCK2/RIO,WP,WG,RN,DEPR,RITX,RINT,RIMP,RIMT
        COMMON/BLOCK3/CONV,HSDN,YHSD,TAXS,SAVG,CONS,TRAF,RIMD,RDUT
        COMMON/BLOCK4/RIMC,CAPF,COSV,CAPUT
        COMMON/BLOCK5/PIMP,PWAG PREN,PDEP,PINT,PTAX
        WRITE(NO,5)
5       FORMAT( / ,130H-----------------------------------BASE YEAR DATA INPUT-
      1----------------------------------------------------------------
      2------------------,//)
        WRITE(NO,6)
```
                                                                              135
                                                                              136
                                                                              137

```
 6    FORMAT(92X,3HSUM,/)
      GO TO 999
C
C READ XXXX-YYYY DEFLATION FACTORS FOR THE I/O ARRAY
C
      WRITE(NO,4)
 4    FORMAT(1X,*DEFLATION FACTORS FOR I/O ARRAY*)
      CALL READV2(FACTR)
C
C DEFLATE I/O ARRAY TO 1XXO LEVELS
C
      WRITE(NO,99)
 99   FORMAT(1X,*DEFLATED I/O ARRAY*)
      CALL DEFLAT(FACTR,RIO)
 999  CONTINUE
C READ BASE YEAR DATA ON I/O MATRIX,WAGES,RENTS AND SCALE WP, WG, AND RE     140
      WRITE(NO,100)
 100  FORMAT(1X,*I/O ARRAY*)
      CALL READM1(RIO)
      WRITE(NO,101)
 101  FORMAT(1X,*PRIVATE WAGES*)
      CALL READMT(WP)
      WRITE(NO,102)
 102  FORMAT(1X,*GOVERMENT WAGES*)
      CALL READMT(WG)
      WRITE(NO,103)
 103  FORMAT(1X,*RENTS*)
      CALL READMT(RN)
C READ BASE YEAR DATA ON DEPRECIATION,TAXES,SUBSIDIES,INTEREST,IMPORTS,      145
C EXPORTS,STOCK CHANGES,INVESTMENT                                          146
      WRITE(NO,104)
 104  FORMAT(1X,*DEPRECIATION IN EACH SECTOR*)
      CALL READV3(DEPR)
      WRITE(NO,106)
 106  FORMAT(1X,*INDIRECT TAXES*)
      CALL READV3(RITX)
      WRITE(NO,107)
 107  FORMAT(1X,*SUBSIDIES*)
      CALL READV3(SUBS)
      WRITE(NO,108)
 108  FORMAT(1X,*INTEREST PAID*)
      CALL READV3(RINT)
```

141

```
      WRITE(NO,109)
  109 FORMAT(1X,*INTERMEDIATE IMPORTS*)
      CALL READV3(RIMP)
      WRITE(NO,110)
  110 FORMAT(1X,*CAPITAL IMPORTS*)
      CALL READV3(RIMC)
      WRITE(NO,111)
  111 FORMAT(1X,*IMPORT DUTY*)
      CALL READV3(RIMT)
      WRITE(NO,112)
  112 FORMAT(1X,*EXPORTS BY SECTOR*)
      CALL READV3(REXP)
      WRITE(NO,113)
  113 FORMAT(1X,*STOCK CHANGE*)
      CALL READV3(STOC)
      WRITE(NO,114)
  114 FORMAT(1X,*INVESTMENT*)
      CALL READV3(RINV)
C READ ACTUAL CAPITAL FORMATION PER SECTOR                           157
      WRITE(NO,115)
  115 FORMAT(1X,*CAPITAL FORMATION (CONSTRUCTION EFFECT)*)            159
      CALL READV3(CAPF)
C READ CONVERSION MATRIX
      WRITE(NO,116)                                                   160
  116 FORMAT(1X,*CONVERSION MATRIX*)
      DO 15 I=1,5
      CALL READV3(DUMMY)
      DO 10 J=1,10
      CONV(J,I)=DUMMY(J)                                             163
   10 CONTINUE                                                        164
   15 CONTINUE                                                        165
C READ HOUSEHOLD NUMBERS,INCOME,TAXES,SAVINGS                        166
      WRITE(NO,117)
  117 FORMAT(1X,*HOUSEHOLD NO.S/INCOME CLASS*)                       167
      CALL READVC(HSDN)
      WRITE(NO,118)
  118 FORMAT(1X,*INCOME /HOUSEHOLD BY INCOME CLASS*)                 168
      READ(NI,16)YHSD
   16 FORMAT(8X,9(1X,F7.1))
      WRITE(NO,17)(ARRAY(I),YHSD(I),I=1,9)                           170
   17 FOPMAT(1X,9H710 Y/HD ,9(A1,F7.1),10X)
      WRITE(NO,119)
```

142

```
119     FORMAT(1X, *TAXES PAID BY INCOME CLASS*)                              172
        CALL READVC(TAXS)
        WRITE(NO,120)
120     FORMAT(1X, *SAVINGS BY INCOME CLASS *)                                173
        CALL READVC(SAVG)                                                     174
C READ ALLOCATION OF CONSUMER SAVING BETWEEN SECTORS
        WRITE(NO,121)
121     FORMAT(1X, *ALLOCATION OF CONSUMER SAVINGS BY SECTOR*)
        CALL READV3(COSV)
C READ CONSUMPTION MATRIX
        WRITE(NO,122)
122     FORMAT(1X, *DIRECT CONSUMPTION MATRIX*)                               177
        DO 20 I=1,4
        CALL READVC(DUMMY)
        DO 18 J=1,10
        CONS(J,I)=DUMMY(J)
18      CONTINUE                                                              180
20      CONTINUE                                                              181
C READ DIRECT CONSUMER IMPORTS AND DUTY                                       182
        WRITE(NO,123)                                                         176
123     FORMAT(1X, *DIRECT CONSUMER IMPORTS*)                                 183
        CALL READVC(RIMD)
        WRITE(NO,124)
124     FORMAT(1X, *DUTY ON DIRECT CONSUMER IMPORTS*)
        CALL RE:JVC(RDUT)                                                     184
C READ TRANSFERS FROM GROUPS F-I TO GROUPS A-E                                185
        WRITE(NO,125)
125     FORMAT(1X, *TRANSFERS*)                                              186
        DO 24 I=1,4                                                           187
        CALL READVC(DUMMY)                                                    188
        DO 22 J=1,9                                                           189
        TRAF(J,I)=DUMMY(J)                                                    190
22      CONTINUE                                                              191
24      CONTINUE                                                              192
C READ GOVERNMENT TO CAPITAL,DEFICIT,LOANS,LOAN SERVICE
        WRITE(NO,126)
126     FORMAT(1X, *GOV.CAP.INVEST., GOV.DEFICIT, GOV.LOANS, GOV.LN.SRV.*
       1* GOV.T ENT SURPL*)
        READ(NI,25)GOVCA,GOVZ,GOVL,GOVLS
25      FORMAT(8X,9(2X,F6.0))                                                 194
        WRITE(NO,26)GOVCA,GOVZ,GOVL,GOVLS                                     195
26      FORMAT(1X,11H1000GOVT CA,F6.0,2HZ ,F6.0,2HL ,F6.0,2ii:5,F6.0)
```

```
C READ IN THE BASE YEAR CAPACITY UTILISATION COEFFICIENT
      WRITE(NO,127)
127   FORMAT(1X,*CAPACITY UTILIZATION*)
      CALL READV2(CAPUT)
C READ IN THE BASE YEAR EMPLOYMENT MATRIX
      WRITE(NO,128)
128   FORMAT(1X,*BASE YEAR EMPLOYMENT MATRIX*)
      DO 30 I=1,10
      CALL READVC(DUMMY)
      DO 31 J=1,9
      EMPLOY(J,I)=DUMMY(J)
31    CONTINUF
30    CONTINU:
      WRITE(NO,28)
28    FORMAT(//,130H---------------------------------------END BASE YEAR DATA IN
     1PUT-----------------------------------------------------------------
     2----------------,//)
      RETURN
      END

      SUBROUTINE BANNER(NPER)
C
C BANNER WRITES GENERAL PROGRAM ID.S
C
      DIMENSION ARRAY(9),SECTOR(10),GO(10),GROW(10)
      COMMON/BLOCK1/ARRAY,SECTOR,GO,NYEAR,NI,NO,NBASE
      WRITE(NO,1)
1     FORMAT(1H1,130H*******************************   **********************************
     1***************************************   ********************************
     2**********,//)
      WRITE(NO,2)
2     FORMAT(40X,34HSIMULATION OF THE ZIMBABWE ECONOMY,//)
      WRITE(NO,3)
3     FORMAT(40X,45HDEVELOPED BY C. SLATER, L. POOK,              ,//)
      WRITE(NO,4)
4     FORMAT(40X,19HDATE - DEC 12, 1976,//)
      WRITE(NO,5) NYEAR, NPER
5     FORMAT(40X,13HBASE YEAR IS ,I4,24H ,SIMULATION TO RUN FOR ,I2,18H
     1CONSECUTIVE YEARS.//)
      WRITE(NO,6)
C     FORMAT(1X ,130H...
     :*****************************************************...
```

144

```
2*************,//)
      RETURN
      END
C  SUBROUTINE BALANCE(TOTCOV,SUBS,STD,REXP,RINV)
      SUBROUTINE BALANCE PROVIDES BASE YEAR BALANCE CHECKS ON THE INPUT DATA
      DIMENSION ARRAY(9),SECTOR(10),GO(10),GROW(10)
      DIMENSION RIO(10,10),WP(9,10),WG(9,10),RN(9,10)
      DIMENSION DEPR(10),RITX(10),RINT(10),RIMP(10),RINT(10)
      DIMENSION CONV(10,5),HSDN(9),YHSD(9),TAXS(9),SAVG(9)
      DIMENSION CONS(10,4),TRAF(9,4),RIMD(9),RDUT(9)
      DIMENSION RIMC(10),CAPF(10),COSV(10),CAPUT(10)
      DIMENSION PIMP(10),PWAG(10),PREN(10),PDEP(10),PINT(10)
      DIMENSION PTAX(10),CAPAC(10)
      DIMENSION CONST(10),FD(10),WAGES(9),RENTS(9),FACINF(9),YOLD(9)
      DIMENSION CONSIM(10),CONDEM(10),PRICE(10),SUBS(10),TOTCOV(9)
      DIMENSION EMPLOY(9,10)
      DIMENSION BASEGO(10)
      DIMENSION GOLD(10)
      DIMENSION REXP(10),RINV(10),STOC(10)
      DIMENSION DUMMY(10)
      DIMENSION            TOTINC(9),TOTPVT(10),TOTCOS(4),TOTPCO(10)
      COMMON/BLOCK1/ARRAY,SECTOR,GO,NYEAR,NI,NO,NBASE
      COMMON/BLOCK2/RIO,WP,WG,RN,DEPR,RITX,RINT,RIMP,RIMT
      COMMON/BLOCK3/CONV,HSDN,YHSD,TAXS,SAVG,CONS,TRAF,RIMC,RDUT
      COMMON/BLOCK4/RIMC,CAPF,COSV,CAPUT
      COMMON/BLOCK5/PIMP,PWAG,PREN,PDEP,PINT,PTAX
      WRITE(NO,28)
   28 FORMAT(1H1,130H-----------------------------------BASE YEAR BALANCE CHE
     1CKS----------------,//)
C  THREE WAY BALANCE CHECK FOR HOUSEHOLD INCOME
      DO 30 I=1,9
      TOTINC(I)=YHSD(I)*HSDN(I)
   30 CONTINUE
      WRITE(NO,35)ARRAY,TOTINC
   35 FORMAT(15X,9(4X,A1,4X)//11H 'HSD*Y/HSD,4X,9F9.0/)
      DO 50 I=1,9
      TOTINC(I)=0
      DO 40 J=1,10
      TOTINC(I)=TOTINC(I)+WP(I,J)+WG(I,J)+RN(I,J)
   40 CONTINUE
```

205
206
207
208
209
210
211
212

214
215

145

```
      50  CONTINUE                                                        216
          DO 70 I=1,9                                                     217
          DO 60 J=1,4                                                     218
          TOTINC(I)=TOTINC(I)+TRAF(I,J)                                   219
      60  CONTINUE                                                        220
      70  CONTINUE                                                        221
          WRITE(NO,100)TOTINC                                             222
     100  FORMAT(15H WAG+REN+-TRANS,9F9.0/)                               223
          DO 120 I=1,9                                                    224
          TOTINC(I)=TAXS(I)+SAVG(I)+RIMD(I)                               225
          DO 110 J=1,4                                                    226
          TOTINC(I)=TOTINC(I)+CONS(I,J)                                   227
     110  CONTINUE                                                        228
     120  CONTINUE                                                        229
          WRITE(NO,130)TOTINC                                             230
     130  FORMAT(15H TAX+SAV+CONSUM,9F9.0/)                               231
      C CHECK THAT HOUSEHOLD CONSUMPTION EQUALS AMOUNTS SHOWN IN CONV MATRIX  232
          DO 150 J=1,4                                                    233
          TOTCOS(J)=0                                                     234
          DO 140 I=1,9                                                    235
          TOTCOS(J)=TOTCOS(J)+CONS(I,J)                                   236
     140  CONTINUE                                                        237
     150  CONTINUE                                                        238
          DO 170 J=1,5                                                    239
          TOTCOV(J)=0                                                     240
          DO 160 I=1,10                                                   242
          TOTCOV(J)=TOTCOV(J)+CONV(I,J)                                   243
     160  CONTINUE                                                        244
     170  CONTINUE                                                        245
          WRITE(NO,180)((TOTCOS(J),TOTCOV(J)),J=1,4)                      246
     180  FORMAT(/22H HOUSEHOLD CONSUMPTION/14X,23HFROM CONSUMPTION MATRIX,  247
         15X,22HFROM CONVERSION MATRIX/12H TRADITIONAL,9X,F8.0,20X,F8.0/ 248
         210H UTILITIES,11X,F8.0,20X,F8.0/9H COMMERCE,12X,F8.0,20X,F8.0/ 249
         39H SERVICES,12X,F8.0,20X,F8.0//)                               250
      C CHECK THAT CONSUMPTION OF 10SECTORS IS EQUAL TO INPUTS+IMPORTS+WAGES  251
      C +RENTS-DEPR+INTEREST+IND.TAXES-SUBSIDIES-STOCKC-EXPORTS-INTERM.USE 252
      C -INVESTMENT                                                       254
          DO 210 I=1,10
          TOTPVT(I)=0
          DO 200 J=1,10
          TOTPVT(I)=TOTPVT(I)+QIO(I,J)-PIO(J,I)
     200  CONTINUE                                                        257
```

146

```
         DO 205 J=1,9
         TOTPVT(I)=TOTPVT(I)+WP(J,I)+WG(J,I)+RN(J,I)
205      CONTINUE
         TOTPVT(I)=TOTPVT(I)+RIMP(I)+DEPR(I)+RINT(I)+RITX(I)-SUBS(I)    258
         TOTPVT(I)=TOTPVT(I)+RIMC(I)                                    259
         TOTPVT(I)=TOTPVT(I)-STOC(I)-REXP(I)-RINV(I)                    260
210      CONTINUE                                                       261
         DO 230 I=1,10
         TOTPCO(I)=0                                                    263
         DO 220 J=1,5                                                   264
         TOTPCO(I)=TOTPCO(I)+CONV(I,J)                                  265
220      CONTINUE                                                       266
230      CONTINUE                                                       267
         WRITE(NO,240)                                                  268
240      FORMAT(50X,32HPRIVATE CONSUMPTION OF 10SECTORS/48X,4HTRAD,3X,6HMOD  26
        1AGR,2X,5HMANUF,4X,3H8+C,5X,4HUTIL,2X,8HCOMMERCE,2X,5HTRANS,3X,4HSV   270
        2CS,4X,3HGOV,6X,6HMINING//)
         WRITE(NO,250)
250      FORMAT(46H AS SUM OF INPUT+IMPORTS+WAGES+RENTS+DEPR+INT.)       272
         WRITE(NO,260)TOTPVT                                            273
260      FORMAT(46H +IND.TAXES-SUBS-STOCKC-EXPORTS-INTERM.-INVEST,10F8.0/)  274
         WRITE(NO,270)TOTPCO
270      FORMAT(14X,22HFROM CONVERSION MATRIX,10X,10F8.0)               276
         WRITE(NO,310)
310      FORMAT(//, 130H---------------------------------END BALANCE CHECKS---
        1-------------------------------------------------
        2-----------------,//,1H1)                                      278
         RETURN                                                         279
         END

C THIS SUBROUTINE COEFF(TOTCOV,CAPAC,EMPLOY)
C THIS SUBROUTINE CONVERTS THE BASE PERIOD I/O DATA AND HOUSEHOLD
C CONSUMPTION DATA INTO SCALED COEFFICIENTS FOR USE IN LATER YEARS    303
      DIMENSION ARRAY(9),SECTOR(10),GO(10),GROW(10)                    304
      DIMENSION RIO(10,10), WP(9,10), WG(9,10), RN(9,10)               305
      DIMENSION DEPR(10), RITX(10), RINT(10), RIMP(10), RIMT(10)
      DIMENSION CONV(10,5), HSDN(9), YHSD(9), TAXS(9), SAVG(9)
      DIMENSION CONS(10,4), TRAF(9,4), RIMD(9), RDUT(9)
      DIMENSION RIMC(10), CAPF(10), COSV(10), CAPUT(10)
      DIMENSION PIMP(10), PWAG(10), PREN(10), PDEP(10), PINT(10)
      DIMENSION PTAX(10), CAPAC(10)
      DIMENSION CONST(10), FD(10), WAGES(9), RENTS(9), FAC(NF(9),YOLD(9)
```

147

```
      DIMENSION CONSIM(10), CONDEM(10), PRICE(10), SUBS(10), TOTCOV(9)
      DIMENSION EMPLOY(9,10)
      DIMENSION BASEGO(10)
      DIMENSION GOLD(10)
      DIMENSION REXP(10), RINV(10), STOC(10)
      DIMENSION TOTINC(9)
      COMMON/BLOCK1/ARRAY,SECTOR,GO,NYEAR,NI,NO,NBASE
      COMMON/BLOCK2/RIO,WP,WG,RN,DEPR,RITX,RINT,RIMP,RIMT
      COMMON/BLOCK3/CONV,HSDN,YHSD,TAXS,SAVG,CONS,TRAF,RIMC,RDUT
      COMMON/BLOCK4/RIMC,CAPF,COSV,CAPUT
      COMMON/BLOCK5/PIMP,PWAG,PREN,PDEP,PINT,PTAX
C CALCULATE GROSS OUTPUT OF TEN SECTORS
      DO 20 I=1,10
      GO(I)=0.
      DO 10 J=1,10
      GO(I)=GO(I)+RIO(I,J)
   10 CONTINUE
      GO(I)=GO(I)+RIMP(I)+DEPR(I)+RINT(I)+RITX(I)
   20 CONTINUE
      DO 24 I=1,10
      DO 26 J=1,9
      GO(I)=GO(I)      +WP(J,I)+WG(J,I)+RN(J,I)
   26 CONTINUE
   24 CONTINUE
      WRITE(NO,22)NYEAR
   22 FORMAT(//I5,28H OUTPUT AND TECHNICAL COEFFS//)
      WRITE(NO,25)GO
   25 FORMAT(29H GROSS OUTPUT OF TEN SECTORS /10F8.0/)
C CALCULATE COEFFS FOR DUTY ON 10 SECTOR INTERMED AND CAP IMPORTS
      DO 28 I=1,10
      TIMPTI=RIMP(I)+RIMC(I)
      IF(TIMPTI.LT.1.0)TIMPTI=1.0
      RIMP(I)=RIMP(I)/TIMPTI
      RIMT(I)=RIMT(I)/TIMPTI
   28 CONTINUE
C CALCULATE TCS BY SCALING WITH RESPECT TO GROSS OUTPUT
      DO 40 I=1,10
      IF(GO(I).LT.1.0)GO(I)=1.0
      RIMP(I)=RIMP(I)/GO(I)
      DEPR(I)=DEPR(I)/GO(I)
      RINT(I)=RINT(I)/GO(I)
      RITX(I)=RITX(I)/GO(I)
      DO 30 J=1,10
```

017
018

020

320

323
324
325

326
327
328

332
333
334
335
336

338
339
340
341

```
         RIO(I,J)=RIO(I,J)/GO(I)                                            343
  30  CONTINUE                                                              348
  40  CONTINUE                                                              349
      DO 35 I=1,9
      DO 36 J=1,10
      WP(I,J)=WP(I,J)/GO(J)                                                 344
      WG(I,J)=WG(I,J)/GO(J)                                                 345
      RN(I,J)=RN(I,J)/GO(J)                                                 346
      EMPLOY(I,J)=EMPLOY(I,J)/GO(J)                                         347
  36  CONTINUE
  35  CONTINUE
      WRITE(NO,50)SECTOR
  50  FORMAT(20X,23H TECHNICAL COEFFICIENTS/10X,10A6/)                      350
      WRITE(NO,60)RIO
  60  FORMAT(10H INTERMED ,10F6.4/(10X,10F6.4/))                            352
      WRITE(NO,65)ARRAY
  65  FORMAT(10X,9(5X,A1,4X)/)
      WRITE(NO,70)WP
  70  FORMAT(10H PRVWAGES , 9F6.4/(10X, 9F6.4/))                            354
      WRITE(NO,80)WG
  80  FORMAT(10H GOVWAGES , 9F6.4/(10X, 9F6.4/))                            356
      WRITE(NO,90)RN
  90  FORMAT(6H RENTS,4X, 9F6.4/(10X, 9F6.4/))                              358
      WRITE(NO,100)RIMP,DEPR,RINT,RITX
 100  FORMAT(10H IMPORTS  ,10F6.4/10H DEPRCION ,10F6.4/10H INTEREST         360
     19F6.4/10H INDTAXES ,10F6.4)
C  CALCULATE CAPITAL IMPORTS COEFF AS FUNCTION OF CAPITAL FORMATION
      DO 110 I=1,10                                                         363
      IF(CAPF(I).LT.1.0)CAPF(I)=1.0
      RIMC(I)=RIMC(I)/CAPF(I)
 110  CONTINUE                                                              365
C  CALCULATE THE CAPACITY OF THE TEN SECTORS                                366
      DO 120 I=1,10
      IF(CAPUT(I).LT.1.0)CAPUT(I)=1.0                                       369
      CAPAC(I)=GO(I)/CAPUT(I)                                               370
 120  CONTINUE                                                             371
      WRITE(NO,125)NYEAR,SECTOR,CAPAC
 125  FORMAT(I5,24H CAPACITY OF EACH SECTOR/10(2X,A6,2X)/:0F10.0/)
C  CALCULATE COEFFICIENTS FOR DUTY ON DIRECT CONSUMER IMPOR!S
      DO 140 I=1,9                                                          373
      IF(RIMD(I).LT.1.0)RIMD(I)=1.0                                         374
      RDUT(I)=RDUT(I)/RIMD(I)                                               375
                                                                           376
```

149

```
      140 CONTINUE
C CALCULATE COEFFICIENTS FOR HOUSEHOLD CONSUMPTION
          DO 150 I=1,9
          TOTINC(I)=YHSD(I)*HSDN(I)
      150 CONTINUE
          DO 170 I=1,9
          IF(TOTINC(I).LT.1.0)TOTINC(I)=1.0
          TAXS(I)=TAXS(I)/TOTINC(I)
          SAVG(I)=SAVG(I)/TOTINC(I)
          RIMD(I)=RIMD(I)/TOTINC(I)
      170 CONTINUE
          DO 165 I=1,9
          DO 160 J=1,4
          CONS(I,J)=CONS(I,J)/TOTINC(I)
      160 CONTINUE
      165 CONTINUE
C CALCULATE COEFFICIENTS IN CONVERSION MATRIX
          DO 190 I=1,5
          IF(TOTCOV(I).LT.1.0)TOTCOV(I)=1.0
          DO 180 J=1,10
          CONV(J,I)=CONV(J,I)/TOTCOV(I)
      180 CONTINUE
      190 CONTINUE
C CALCULATE COEFFICIENTS FOR ALLOCATION OF CONSUMER SAVINGS TO10 SECTORS
          CONSAV=0
          DO 200 I=1,10
          CONSAV=CONSAV+COSV(I)
      200 CONTINUE
          IF(CONSAV.LT.1.0)CONSAV=1.0
          DO 210 I=1,10
          COSV(I)=COSV(I)/CONSAV
      210 CONTINUE
          RETURN
          END
      SUBROUTINE INVEST(CAPAC,CAPIMD,EMPLOY)
C THIS SUBROUTINE MAKES AMENDMENTS TO TECHNICAL COEFFICIENTS AND
C CAPACITY DUE TO CAPITAL INVESTMENT.ALSO CALCULATES CAP IMPORTS,DUTY.
      DIMENSION ARRAY(9),SECTOR(10),GO(10),GROW(10)
      DIMENSION RIO(10,10),WP(9,10),WG(9,10),RN(9,10)
      DIMENSION DEPR(10),RITX(10),RINT(10),RIMP(10),RIMT(10)
      DIMENSION CONV(10,5),HSDN(9),YHSD(9),TAXS(9),SAVG(9)
```

```
      DIMENSION CONS(10,4), TRAF(9,4), RIMD(9,), RDUT(9)
      DIMENSION RIMC(10), CAPF(10), COSV(10), CAPUT(10)
      DIMENSION PIMP(10), PWAG(10), PREN(10), PDEP(10), PINT(10)
      DIMENSION PTAX(10), CAPAC(10)
      DIMENSION CONST(10), FD(10), WAGES(9), RENTS(9), FAC,NF(9),YOLD(9)
      DIMENSION CONSIM(10), CONDEM(10), PRICE(10), SUBS(10), TOTCOV(9)
      DIMENSION EMPLOY(9,10)
      DIMENSION BASEGO(10)
      DIMENSION GOLD(10)
      DIMENSION REXP(10), RINV(10), STOC(10)
      DIMENSION CAPNET(10), CAPR(10)
      DIMENSION CAPRAT(10)
      DIMENSION TCIN(10),TCIM(10),TCWA(10),TCRE(10),TCIT(1C),TCDE(10)
      DIMENSION TCTX(10)
      DIMENSION PCTREN(10),PCTINP(10),PCTIMP(10),PCTDEP(10),PCTINT(10)
      DIMENSION PCTITX(10),PCTWAG(10)
      COMMON/BLOCK1/ARRAY,SECTOR,GO,NYEAR,NI,NO,NBASE
      COMMON/BLOCK2/RIO,WP,WG,RN,DEPR,RITX,RINT,RIMP,RIMT
      COMMON/BLOCK3/CONV,HSDN,YIISD,TAXS,SAVG,CONS,TRAF,RIMD,RDUT
      COMMON/BLOCK4/RIMC,CAPF,COSV,CAPUT
      COMMON/BLOCK5/PIMP,PWAG,PREN,PDEP,PINT,PTAX
    C CALCULATE TOTAL CAPITAL IMPORTS AND DUTY                              017
      CAPIMP=0.                                                            018
      CAPIMD=0
      DO 10 I=1,10                                                         020
      CAPIMP=CAPIMP+CAPF(I)*RIMC(I)                                        418
      CAPIMD=\PIMD+CAPF(I)*RIMC(I)*RIMT(I)
   10 CONTINUE                                                             420
      WRITE(NO,20)CAPIMP,CAPIMD
   20 FORMAT(18H CAPITAL IMPORTS =,F9.0,7H DUTY =,F9.0/)                   422
    C READ IN CAPITAL CAPACITY RATIOS FOR 10 SECTORS                       423
      CALL READV5(CAPRAT)                                                  424
    C CALCULATE NEW CAPACITY OF 10 SECTORS                                 425
      DO 40 I=1,10                                                         426
      CAPNET(I)=CAPF(I)-DEPR(I)
      CAPAC(I)=CAPAC(I)+CAPNET(I)/CAPRAT(I)                                432
   40 CONTINUE                                                             433
      WRITE(NO,50)NYEAR,SECTOR,CAPAC                                       434
   50 FORMAT(I5,27H PROVISIONAL CAPACITY VALUE/10(2X,A6,2X')/10F10.0/)     435
    C READ IN HOW 10 MILLION UNITS OF INVESTMENT IN EACH SECTOR AFFECTS THE 437
    C TECHNICAL COEFFICIENTS OF INPUTS,INTERMEDIATE IMPORTS,WAGES,RENTS,   438
    C INTEREST,DEPRECIATION AND INDIRECT TAXES                            439
```

151

```
      CALL READV6(TCIN)
      CALL READV6(TCIM)
      CALL READV6(TCWA)
      CALL READV6(TCRE)
      CALL READV6(TCIT)
      CALL READV6(TCDE)
      CALL READV6(TCTX)
      WRITE(NO,65)SECTOR                                              442
   65 FORMAT(39H MATRIX OF TECHNICAL COEFFICIENT CHANGE/8X,10(1X,A6)/)
      WRITE(NO,70)TCIN,TCIM,TCWA,TCRE,TCIT,TCDE,TCTX                  444
   70 FORMAT(8H INPUTS ,10F7.4/8H IMPORTS,10F7.4/8H WAGES  ,10F7.4/
     18H RENTS  ,10F7.4/8H INTREST,10F7.4/8H DEPRECN,10F7.4/8H TAXES
     210F7.4/)
    C CALCULATE THE CHANGES IN TECHNICAL COEFFICIENTS INDUCED BY INVESTMENT 447
      DO 100 I=1,10
      CAPR(I)=CAPF(I)/10000.
      CHAWAG=1-CAPR(I)+CAPR(I)*TCWA(I)                                449
      CHAREN=1-CAPR(I)+CAPR(I)*TCRE(I)                                454
      CHAINP=1-CAPR(I)+CAPR(I)*TCIN(I)                                455
      CHAIMP=1-CAPR(I)+CAPR(I)*TCIM(I)                                456
      CHADEP=1-CAPR(I)+CAPR(I)*TCDE(I)
      CHAINT=1-CAPR(I)+CAPR(I)*TCIT(I)
      CHAITX=1-CAPR(I)+CAPR(I)*TCTX(I)
      PCTWAG(I)=(1-CHAWAG)*100.
      PCTREN(I)=(1-CHAREN)*100.
      PCTINP(I)=(1-CHAINP)*100.
      PCTIMP(I)=(1-CHAIMP)*100.
      PCTDEP(I)=(1-CHADEP)*100.
      PCTINT(I)=(1-CHAINT)*100.
      PCTITX(I)=(1-CHAITX)*100.
      RIMP(I)=RIMP(I)*CHAIMP
      DEPR(I)=DEPR(I)*CHADEP
      RINT(I)=RINT(I)*CHAINT
      RITX(I)=RITX(I)*CHAITX
      DO 90 J=1,10
      RIO(I,J)=RIO(I,J)*CHAINP
   90 CONTINUE                                                        458
      DO 91 J=1,9                                                     463
      WP(J,I)=WP(J,I)*CHAWAG                                          459
      WG(J,I)=WG(J,I)*CHAWAG                                          460
      RN(J,I)=RN(J,I)*CHAREN                                          461
      EMPLCY(J,I)=EMPLOY(J,I)*CHAWAG                                  462
```

152

```
 91   CONTINUE
100   CONTINUE
      WRITE(NO,105) SECTOR
      WRITE(NO,110)PCTWAG,PCTREN,PCTINP,PCTIMP,PCTINT,PCTITX
105   FORMAT(//70H PERCENT CHANGES INDUCED IN TECHNICAL COEFFICIENTS DUE
     1 TO ABOVE MATRIX/8X,10(1X,A6))
110   FORMAT (/8H WAGES   ,10F7.2/8H RENTS  ,10F7.2/8H INPUTS ,10F7.2/
     18H IMPORTS,10F7.2/8H DEPREC ,10F7.2/8H INTERST,10F7.2/8H TAXES
     210F7.2/)
      WRITE(NO,120)SECTOR,RIO,WP,WG,RN
120   FORMAT(//34H AMENDED TCS INDUCED BY INVESTMENT/10X,10A6/10H I/O CO
     1EFF/10(10X,10F6.4/)/10H PRIV WAGE/10(10X,  9F6.4/)/10H GOVT WAGE/
     210(10X,  9F6.4/)/6H RENTS/10(10X,  9F6.4/))
      WRITE(NO,130)RIMP,DEPR,RINT,RITX
130   FORMAT(/10H INT IMPTS/10X,10F6.4/13H DEPRECIATION/10X,10F6.4/
     110H INTEREST /10X,10F6.4/10H IND TAXES/10X,10F6.4//)
      RETURN
      END

C THIS SUBROUTINE READS IN PRICE CHANGES IN IMPORTS,WAGES,RENTS,
C DEPRECIATION,INTEREST AND TAXES. IT THEN CALCULATES THE NEW PRICE
C OF OUTPUT IN THE 10 SECTORS
      SUBROUTINE PRICEC(PRICE,CAPAC,GOLD)
      DIMENSION ARRAY(9),SECTOR(10),GO(10),GROW(10)
      DIMENSION RIO(10,10), WP(9,10), WG(9,10), RN(9,10)
      DIMENSION DEPR(10), RITX(10), RINT(10), RIMP(10), RIMT(10)
      DIMENSION CONV(10,5), HSDN(9), YHSD(9), TAXS(9), SAVG(9)
      DIMENSION CONS(10,4), TRAF(9,4), RIMD(9), RDUT(9)
      DIMENSION RIMC(10), CAPF(10), COSV(10), CAPUT(10)
      DIMENSION PIMP(10), PWAG(10), PREN(10), PDEP(10), PINT(10)
      DIMENSION PTAX(10), CAPAC(10)
      DIMENSION CONST(10), FD(10), WAGES(9), RENTS(9), FACINF(9),YOLD(9)
      DIMENSION CONSIM(10), CONDEM(10), PRICE(10), SUBS(10), TOTCOV(9)
      DIMENSION EMPLOY(9,10)
      DIMENSION BASEGO(10)
      DIMENSION GOLD(10)
      DIMENSION REXP(10), RINV(10), STOC(10)
      DIMENSION WAG(10), REN(10), RHS(10), A(100), W(3)
      COMMON/BLOCK1/ARRAY,SECTOR,GO,NYEAR,NI,NO,NBASE
      COMMON/BLOCK2/RIO,WP,WG,RN,DEPR,RITX,RINT,RIMP,RIMT
      COMMON/BLOCK3/CONV,HSDN,YHSD,TAXS,SAVG,CONS,TRAF,RIMD,RDUT
      COMMON/BLOCK4/RIMC,CAPF,COSV,CAPUT
      COMMON/BLOCK5/PIMP,PWAG,PREN,PDEP,PINT,PTAX
```

464

465

469

472
473

474
475
476

017
018

020

```
C READ IN PRICE CHANGES
      CALL READV6(PIMP)
      CALL READV6(PWAG)
      CALL READV6(PREN)
      CALL READV6(PDEP)
      CALL READV6(PINT)
      CALL READV6(PTAX)
      WRITE(NO,8)SECTOR                                                    487
    8 FORMAT(.21H PRICE CHANGES MATRIX/8X,10(2X,A6)/)
      WRITE(NO,10)PIMP,PWAG,PREN,PDEP,PINT,PTAX                            490
   10 FORMAT(8H IMPORTS,10F8.2/8H WAGES   ,10F8.2/8H RENTS  ,10F8.2/       492
     18H DEPRECN.10F8.2/8H INTREST,10F8.2/8H TAXES   ,10F8.2/)
C ADD UP THE TOTAL WAGES AND RENTS COEFFICIENTS FOR EACH SECTOR           495
      DO 20I=1,10
      WAG(I)=0
      REN(I)=0
      DO 15 J=1,9                                                         497
      WAG(I)=WAG(I)+WP(J,I)+WG(J,I)                                       498
      REN(I)=REN(I)+RN(J,I)                                               499
   15 CONTINUE                                                            500
   20 CONTINUE                                                            501
C CALCULATE RIGHT HAND SIDE FOR OUTPUT PRICE DETERMINATION EQUATIONS      502
      DO 40 I=1,10                                                        503
      RHS(I)=RIMP(I)*PIMP(I)+WAG(I)*PWAG(I)+REN(I)*PREN(I)-               504
     1DEPR(I)*PDEP(I)+RINT(I)*PINT(I)+RITX(I)*PTAX(I)
   40 CONTINUE                                                            506
C CALCULATE LHS MATRIX OF COEFF FOR OUTPUT PRICE DETERMINATION EQUATIONS  507
      DO 60 I=1,10                                                        508
      DO 50 J=1,10                                                        509
      K=I+10*(J-1)
      A(K)=-RIO(I,J)
      IF(I.EQ.J)A(K)=1+A(K)                                              513
   50 CONTINUE                                                            514
   60 CONTINUE                                                            515
C SOLVE SIMULTANEOUS EQUATIONS FOR OUTPUT PRICES OF 10 SECTORS AND PRINT  516
      M=10
      N=1
      E=.0000001                                                         519
      CALL FP:GE(M,N,E,A(1),RHS(1),W(1),DET,IRANK,NRR)                    520
      WRITE(NO,70)NYEAR,SECTOR,RHS
   70 FORMAT(/20H OUTPUT PRICE CHANGE,I5/10(2X,A6,2X)/10F10.5)            522
C AMEND CAPACITY OF 10SECTORS IN TERMS OF CURRENT PRICES
```

154

```
      DO 80 I=1,10                                                        526
      PRICE(I)=RHS(I)                                                     527
      CAPAC(I)=CAPAC(I)*PRICE(I)                                          528
      GOLD(I)=GOLD(I)*PRICE(I)                                            529
   80 CONTINUE                                                            530
      WRITE(NO,90)CAPAC                                                   532
   90 FORMAT(/19H NEW CAPACITY VALUE/10F10.0/)                            533
      RETURN
      END

      SUBROUTINE INFLAT(FACINF,YOLD,CONSIM,PRICE)                         535
C THIS SUBROUTINE CALCULATES NEW INCOME/HOUSEHOLD NECESSARY FOR EACH      536
C CONSUMER GROUP A-I TO RETAIN ITS QUANTITY PURCHASED 3AKING PRICE        537
C INFLATION INTO ACCOUNT
      DIMENSION ARRAY(9), SECTOR(10), GO(10), GROW(10)
      DIMENSION RIO(10,10), WP(9,10), WG(9,10), RN(9,10)
      DIMENSION DEPR(10), RITX(10), RINT(10), RIMP(10), RIMT(10)
      DIMENSION CONV(10,5), TRAF(9,4), RIMD(9), RDUT(9), SAVG(9)
      DIMENSION CONS(10,4), HSDN(9), YHSD(9), TAXS(9), RDUT(9)
      DIMENSION RIMC(10), CAPF(10), COSV(10), CAPUT(10)
      DIMENSION PIMP(10), PWAG(10), PREN(10), PDEP(10), PINT(10)
      DIMENSION PTAX(10), CAPAC(10)
      DIMENSION CONST(10), FD(10), WAGES(9), RENTS(9), FACINF(9),YOLD(9)
      DIMENSION CONSIM(10), CONDEM(10), PRICE(10), SUBS(10), TOTCOV(9)
      DIMENSION EMPLOY(9,10)
      DIMENSION BASEGO(10)
      DIMENSION GOLD(10)
      DIMENSION REXP(10), RINV(10), STOC(10)
      DIMENSION TOTCON(10), TOTVAL(10), DCONSP(4),   PRICIM(10)
      COMMON/BLOCK1/ARRAY,SECTOR,GO,NYEAR,NI,NO,NBASE
      COMMON/BLOCK2/RIO,WP,WG,RN,DEPR,RITX,RINT,RIMP,RIMT                  017
      COMMON/BLOCK3/CONV,HSDN,YHSD,TAXS,SAVG,CONS,TRAF,RIMD,RDUT           018
      COMMON/BLOCK4/RIMC,CAPF,COSV,CAPUT
      COMMON/BLOCK5/PIMP,PWAG,PREN,PDEP,PINT,PTAX                          020
C READ IN THE RATIO OF IMPORT PRICE TO HOME PRICE FOR EACH SECTOR         544
      CALL READV7(PRICIM)
    5 FORMAT(8X,F6.4))
C THE CONSUMER PRICE OF THE 10 SECTOR OUTPUTS IS CALCULATED AS A WEIGHTED  548
C AVERAGE OF THE DOMESTIC PRICE AND THE PRICE OF ANY CONSUMPTION IMPORTS   549
C NECESSARY DUE TO CAPACITY SHORTAGE
      DO 10 I=1,10                                                         551
      PRICE(I)=PRICE(I)*(GO(I)+CONSIM(I) PRICIM(I))/(GO(I)+CONSIM(I))      552
   10 CONTINUE
```

```
      WRITE(NO,15)PRICE                                                      553
15 FORMAT(/35H WEIGHTED PRICE OF 10 SECTOR OUTPUT/10F7.4)
C CALCULATE THE PRICE OF 4 DIRECT CONSUMPTION SECTOR GOODS
      DO 20 I=1,4                                                            555
      TOTCON(I)=0                                                            556
      TOTVAL(I)=0                                                            557
      DO 18 J=1,10                                                           558
      TOTCON(I)=TOTCON(I)+CONV(J,I)                                          560
      TOTVAL(I)=TOTVAL(I)+CONV(J,I)*PRICE(J)                                 561
18 CONTINUE                                                                  562
      DCONSP(I)=TOTVAL(I)/TOTCON(I)                                          563
20 CONTINUE                                                                  564
      WRITE(NO,30)DCONSP                                                     565
30 FORMAT(/31H PRICE OF 4 DIRECT CONS SECTORS/5H TRAD,F5.4,5H UTIL,          566
     1F6.4,5H COMM,F6.4,5H SVCS,F6.4/)                                       567
      DO 38 I=1,4                                                            568
      DO 35 J=1,10
      CONV(J,I)=CONV(J,I)*PRICE(J)/DCONSP(I)                                 570
35 CONTINUE                                                                  571
38 CONTINUE                                                                  572
C READ IN PRICE CHANGE DATA ON CONSUMER TAXES,SAVINGS,DIR IMP,TRANSFERS      573
      READ(NI,40)TAXP,SAVP,DIMP,TRANP,SAE                                    574
40 FORMAT(8X,5(2X,F6.4))                                                     575
      WRITE(NO,50)TAXP,SAVP,DIMP,TRANP                                       576
50 FORMAT(/68H PRICE CHANGE IN CONSUMER TAXES,SAVINGS,DIRECT IMPORTS,        577
     1AND TRANSFERS/1X,4F6.4)                                                578
      WRITE(NO,55)SAE                                                        579
55 FORMAT(40H GROWTH IN NEGATIVE SAVINGS TO CLASS E =,F7.4)
C CALCULATE PRICE INFLATION FACTOR FOR EACH INCOME GROUP
      SAVG(5)=SAVG(5)*SAE                                                    582
      DO 80 I=1,9                                                            583
      TAXS(I)=TAXS(I)*TAXP                                                   584
      IF(I.NE.5)SAVG(I)=SAVG(I)*SAVP                                         585
      RIMD(I)=RIMD(I)*DIMP                                                   586
      FACINF(I)=TAXS(I)+SAVG(I)+RIMD(I)                                      587
      DO 70 J=1,4                                                            588
      CONS(I,J)=CONS(I,J)*DCONSP(J)                                          589
      FACINF(I)=FACINF(I)+CONS(I,J)                                          590
70 CONTINUE                                                                  591
80 CONTINUE                                                                  592
      WRITE(NO,85)NYEAR,ARRAY,FACINF                                         593
85 FORMAT(//5,36H INFLATION FACTOR FOR INCOME CLASSES/13X,9(A1,6X)/          594
```

```
      17H FACINF,3X,9F7.4)
C CALCULATE INCREASED TRANSFERS BETWEEN CLASSES              595
      DO 100 I=1,9                                           596
      DO 90 J=1,4                                            597
      TRAF(I,J)=TRAF(I,J)*TRANP                              598
   90 CONTINUE                                               599
  100 CONTINUE                                               600
C CALCULATE NEW INCOME/HOUSEHOLD IN EACH GROUP A-I AND NEW CONSUM COEFFS  601
      DO 120 I=1,9                                           602
      YOLD(I)=YHSD(I)                                        603
      YHSD(I)=YHSD(I)*FACINF(I)                              604
      TAXS(I)=TAXS(I)/FACINF(I)                              605
      SAVG(I)=SAVG(I)/FACINF(I)                              606
      RIMD(I)=RIMD(I)/FACINF(I)                              607
      DO 110 J=1,4                                           608
      CONS(I,J)=CONS(I,J)/FACINF(I)                          609
  110 CONTINUE                                               610
  120 CONTINUE                                               611
C PRINT NEW INCOME HOUSEHOLD IN EACH GROUP A-I               612
      WRITE(NO,140)NYEAR,ARRAY,YHSD                          613
  140 FORMAT(/,I5,31H INCOME PER HOUSEHOLD GROUP A-I/9(3X,A1,3X)/9F7.1)  614
      RETURN                                                 615
      END                                                    616
                                                            617

      SUBROUTINE PAYMNT(WAGES,RENTS,PRICE,TOTITX,TOTIMD,EMPLOY)  618
C THIS SUBROUTINE CALCULATES ALL WAGES,RENTS,ETC. PAYED BY THE NINE  619
C SECTORS.IN ADDITION IT SETS UP THE COEFFICIENTS FOR THE FOLLOWING  620
C YEAR INCLUDING PRICE CHANGES                               621
      DIMENSION ARRAY(9),SECTOR(10),GO(10),GROW(10)
      DIMENSION RIO(10,10), WP(9,10), WG(9,10), RN(9,10)
      DIMENSION DEPR(10), RITX(10), RINT(10), RIMP(10), RINT(10)
      DIMENSION CONV(10,5), HSDN(9), YHSD(9), TAXS(9), SAVG(9)
      DIMENSION CONS(10,4), TRAF(9,4), RIMD(9), RDUT(9)
      DIMENSION RIMC(10), CAPF(10), COSV(10), CAPUT(10)
      DIMENSION PIMP(10), PWAG(10), PREN(10), PDEP(10), PINT(10)
      DIMENSION PTAX(10), CAPAC(10)
      DIMENSION CONST(10), FD(10), WAGES(9), RENTS(9), FACINF(9),YOLD(9)
      DIMENSION CONSIM(10), CONDEM(10), PRICE(10), SUBS(10), TOTCOV(9)
      DIMENSION EMPLOY(9,10)
      DIMENSION BASEGO(10)
      DIMENSION GOLD(10)
      DIMENSION REXP(10), RINV(10), STOC(10)
```

157

```
      COMMON/BLOCK1/ARRAY,SECTOR,GO,NYEAR,NI,NO,NBASE            017
      COMMON/BLOCK2/RIO,WP,WG,RN,DEPR,RITX,RINT,RIMP,RIMT        018
      COMMON/BLOCK3/CONV,HSDN,YHSD,TAXS,SAVG,CONS,TRAF,RIMD,RDUT
      COMMON/BLOCK4/RIMC,CAPF,COSV,CAPUT                         020
      COMMON/BLOCK5/PIMP,PWAG,PREN,PDEP,PINT,PTAX                631
C AMEND COEFFICIENTS OF I/O MATRIX,WAGES,RENTS,IMPORTS,DEPRECIATION  632
C INTEREST,TAXES TO TAKE ACCOUNT OF PRICE CHANGES-ALSO GROSS OUTPUT
      DO 20 I=1,10                                               634
      RIMP(I)=RIMP(I)*PIMP(I)/PRICE(I)                          635
      DEPR(I)=DEPR(I)*PDEP(I)/PRICE(I)                          636
      RINT(I)=RINT(I)*PINT(I)/PRICE(I)                          637
      RITX(I)=RITX(I)*PTAX(I)/PRICE(I)                          638
      GO(I)=GO(I)*PRICE(I)                                      639
      CHAWAG=PWAG(I)/PRICE(I)                                   640
      CHAREN=PREN(I)/PRICE(I)
      DO 10 J=1,10                                              642
      RIO(I,J)=RIO(I,J)*PRICE(J)/PRICE(I)                       647
   10 CONTINUE
      DO 15 J=1,9                                               643
      WP(J,I)=WP(J,I)*CHAWAG                                    644
      WG(J,I)=WG(J,I)*CHAWAG                                    645
      RN(J,I)=RN(J,I)*CHAREN                                    646
      EMPLOY(J,I)=EMPLOY(J,I)/PRICE(I)
   15 CONTINUE                                                  648
   20 CONTINUE                                                  649
C CALCULATE TOTAL WAGES AND RENTS TO INCOME GROUPS A-I ALSO TOTAL TAXES,  650
C INTERMEDIATE IMPORTS AND DUTY. PRINT THESE OUT              651
      TOTIMD=0                                                  652
      TOTITX=0                                                  653
      TOTIMP=0
      DO 40 I=1,10                                              657
      TOTITX=TOTITX+RITX(I)*GO(I)                               658
      TOTIMP=TOTIMP+RIMP(I)*GO(I)                               659
      TOTIMD=TOTIMD+RIMT(I)*GO(I)*RIMT(I)                       664
   40 CONTINUE
      DO 90 I=1,9                                               655
      WAGES(I)=0                                                656
      RENTS(I)=0
   90 CONTINUE
      DO 30 J=1,9
      DO 35 I=1,10
      WAGES(J)=WAGES(J)+GO(I)*(WP(J,I)+WG(J,I))
```

```
   35    RENTS(J)=RENTS(J)+GO(I)*RN(J,I)
   30    CONTINUE
         WRITE(NO,50)NYEAR,ARRAY                                          663
   50    FORMAT(/I5,37H WAGES AND RENTS TO INCOME GROUPS A-I/9(4X,A1,4X)/) 665
         WRITE(NO,60)WAGES,RENTS                                          667
   60    FORMAT(9(2X,F7.0))
         WRITE(NO,70)TOTITX                                               669
   70    FORMAT(31H TOTAL BUSINESS INDIRECT TAX = ,F9.0)                  671
         WRITE(NO,80)TOTIMP,TOTIMD                                        6
   80    FORMAT(30H TOTAL INTERMEDIATE IMPORTS = ,F9.0,7H DUT: =,F9.0)    673
         RETURN                                                          674
         END

         SUBROUTINE REDIS(WAGES,RENTS,FACINC,YOLD)
C THIS SUBROUTINE USES DATA ON POPULATION INCREASE,MIGRATION AND INCOME
C TO REDISTRIBUTE TOTAL POPULATION WITHIN INCOME CLASSES
         DIMENSION ARRAY(9),SECTOR(10),GO(10),GROW(10)                   676
         DIMENSION RIO(10,10), WP(9,10), WG(9,10), RN(9,10)              677
         DIMENSION DEPR(10), RITX(10), RINT(10), RIMP(10), RINT(10)
         DIMENSION CONV(10,5), HSDN(9), YHSD(9), TAXS(9), SAVG(9)
         DIMENSION CONS(10,4), TRAF(9,4), RIMD(9), RDUT(9)
         DIMENSION RIMC(10), CAPF(10), COSV(10), CAPUT(10)
         DIMENSION PIMP(10), PWAG(10), PREN(10), PDEP(10), PINT(10)
         DIMENSION PTAX(10), CAPAC(10)
         DIMENSION CONST(10), FD(10), WAGES(9), RENTS(9), FACINCF(9),YOLD(9)
         DIMENSION CONSIM(10), CONDEM(10), PRICE(10), SUBS(10), TOTCOV(9)
         DIMENSION EMPLOY(9,10)
         DIMENSION BASEGO(10)
         DIMENSION GOLD(10)
         DIMENSION REXP(10), RINV(10), STOC(10)
         DIMENSION TRANS(9), TNEW(9), TOLDIN(9), FACINC(9), CHAPOP(9)
         DIMENSION TNEWIN(9)
         COMMON/BLOCK1/ARRAY,SECTOR,GO,NYEAR,NI,NO,NBASE                  017
         COMMON/BLOCK2/RIO,WP,WG,RN,DEPR,RITX,RINT,RIMP,RIMT             018
         COMMON/BLOCK3/CONV,HSDN,YHSD,TAXS,SAVG,CONS,TRAF,RIMD,RDUT
         COMMON/BLOCK4/RIMC,CAPF,COSV,CAPUT
         COMMON/BLOCK5/PIMP,PWAG,PREN,PDEP,PINT,PTAX                      020
C CALCULATE INTER-GROUP TRANSFERS FOR EACH OF CLASSES A-I
         DO 20 I=1,9                                                      683
         TRANS(I)=0                                                       684
         DO 10 J=1,4                                                      685
                                                                         686
```

159

```
      TRANS(I)=TRANS(I)+TRAF(I,J)                                     689
   10 CONTINUE                                                        690
   20 CONTINUE                                                        691
C CALCULATE NEW INCOME FOR CLASSES A-I AND CHANGE FROM OLD INCOME     692
      DO 30 I=1,9                                                     693
      IF(NYEAR.EQ.1972)TOLDIN(I)=YOLD(I) HSDN(I)                      694
      TNEWIN(1)=WAGES(I)+RENTS(I)+TRANS(I)                            695
      FACINC(I)=TNEWIN(I)/TOLDIN(I)                                   696
   30 CONTINUE                                                        697
      WRITE(NO,35)ARRAY,TOLDIN,TNEWIN,FACINC                          698
   35 FORMAT(/13X,9(A1,6X)/7H OLDINC,3X,9F7.0/7H NEWINC,3X,9F7.0/     699
     17H FACINC,3X,9F7.4/)                                            700
      DO 40 I=1,9                                                     701
      TOLDIN(I)=TNEWIN(I)                                             702
   40 CONTINUE                                                        703
C READ IN POPULATION GROWTH FACTOR AND RURAL URBAN MIGRATION FACTOR   704
C CALCULATE FACTORS FOR POP GROWTH IN RURAL AND URBAN AREAS           705
      READ(NI,50)POPTOT,POPURB                                        706
   50 FORMAT(15X,F6.3,7X,F6.3)                                        707
      WRITE(NO,60)POPTOT,POPURB                                       708
   60 FORMAT(16H POPCHANGE TOTAL,F7.3,6H URBAN,F7.3/)                 709
      RURPOP=HSDN(1)+HSDN(2)+HSDN(3)+HSDN(4)                          710
      URBPOP=HSDN(5)+HSDN(6)+HSDN(7)+HSDN(8)+HSDN(9)                  711
      POPRUR=POPTOT-URBPOP*(POPURB-POPTOT)/RURPOP                     712
C FIRST ATTEMPT AT REDISTRIBUTION OF RURAL INCOME CLASSES BY TRANSFERS 713
C OF POPULATION BETWEEN CLASSES DEPENDENT ON INCOME AND INFLATION CHANGE 714
      CHAPOP(1)=HSDN(1)*0.5*(FACINC(1)-FACINF(1))                     715
      CHAPOP(2)=HSDN(2)*0.5*(FACINC(2)-FACINF(2))                     716
      CHAPOP(3)=HSDN(3)*0.1*(FACINC(3)-FACINF(3))                     717
      DCHMAX=HSDN(4)*0.3                                              718
      IF(CHAPOP(3).GT.DCHMAX)CHAPOP(3)=DCHMAX                         719
      A=-CHAPOP(3)                                                    720
      IF(A.GT.DCHMAX)CHAPOP(3)=-DCHMAX                                721
      HSDN(1)=HSDN(1)-CHAPOP(1)+RURPOP*(POPRUR-1)                     722
      HSDN(2)=HSDN(2)+CHAPOP(1)-CHAPOP(2)                             723
      HSDN(3)=HSDN(3)+CHAPOP(2)-CHAPOP(3)                             724
      HSDN(4)=HSDN(4)+CHAPOP(3)                                       725
C NOW MAKE FINAL CORRECTION ON TOTAL INCOME BY TRANSFER OF PEOPLE FROM 726
C CLASSES 4 AND 3 TO CLASS 1 OR CLASS 1 TO CLASS 4                    727
      PROTOT=0                                                        728
      ACTTOT=0
      DO 80 I=1,4
```

```
          PROTOT=PROTOT+HSDN(I)*YHSD(I)                                    729
          ACTTOT=ACTTOT+TNEWIN(I)                                         730
   80 CONTINUE                                                             731
      TDA=(PROTOT-ACTTOT)/(YHSD(4)-YHSD(1))                               732
      ADMAX=0.3*HSDN(4)                                                   733
      TAD=TDA                                                             734
      IF(TDA.LE.ADMAX.AND.TAD.LE.ADMAX)GO TO 85                          735
      TDA=ADMAX                                                          736
      IF(TAD.GT.0.0)TDA=-ADMAX                                           737
      PROTOT=PROTOT-TDA*(YHSD(4)-YHSD(1))                                738
      TCA=(PROTOT-ACTTOT)/(YHSD(3)-YHSD(1))                              739
      HSDN(1)=HSDN(1)+TCA                                                740
      HSDN(3)=HSDN(3)-TCA                                                741
   85 HSDN(1)=HSDN(1)+TDA                                                742
      HSDN(4)=HSDN(4)-TDA                                                743
      WRITE(NO,90)(ARRAY(I),I=1,4),(HSDN(I),I=1,4)                       744
   90 FORMAT(28H NEW RURAL HOUSEHOLD NUMBERS/4(3X,A1,3X)/4F7.1/)         745
C FIRST ATTEMT AT REDISTRIBUTION OF URBAN INCOME CLASSES BY TRANSFERS    746
C OF POPULATION BETWEEN CLASSES DEPENDENT ON INCOME AND INFLATION CHANGE 747
      CHAPOP(5)=HSDN(5)*(FACINC(5)-FACINF(5))                            748
      CHAPOP(6)=HSDN(6)*0.5*(FACINC(6)-FACINF(6))                        749
      CHAPOP(7)=HSDN(7)*0.5*(FACINC(7)-FACINF(7))                        750
      CHAPOP(8)=HSDN(8)*0.05*(FACINC(8)-FACINF(8))                       751
      CHIMAX=HSDN(9)*0.3                                                 752
      IF(CHAPOP(8).GT.CHIMAX)CHAPOP(8)=CHIMAX                            753
      A=-CHAPOP(8)                                                       754
      IF(A.GT.CHIMAX)CHAPOP(8)=-CHIMAX                                   755
      HSDN(5)=HSDN(5)-CHAPOP(5)+URBPOP*(POPURB-1)                        756
      HSDN(6)=HSDN(6)+CHAPOP(5)-CHAPOP(6)                                757
      HSDN(7)=HSDN(7)+CHAPOP(6)-CHAPOP(7)                                758
      HSDN(8)=HSDN(8)+CHAPOP(7)-CHAPOP(8)                                759
      HSDN(9)=HSDN(9)+CHAPOP(8)                                          760
C NOW MAKE FINAL CORRECTION ON TOTAL INCOME BY TRANSFER OF PEOPLE FROM   761
C CLASSES 9 AND 8 TO CLASS 5 OR CLASS 5 TO CLASS 9                       762
      PROTOT=0                                                           763
      ACTTOT=0                                                           764
      DO 100 I=5,9                                                       765
      PROTOT=PROTOT+HSDN(I)*YHSD(I)                                      766
      ACTTOT=ACTTOT+TNEWIN(I)                                            767
  100 CONTINUE                                                            768
      TIE=(PROTOT-ACTTOT)/(YHSD(9)-YHSD(5))
      EIMAX=0.3*HSDN(9)
```

161

```
        TEI=-TIE
        IF(TIE.LE.EIMAX.AND.TEI.LE.EIMAX)GO TO 105                       771
        TIE=EIMAX                                                        772
        IF(TEI.GT.0.0)TIE=-EIMAX                                         773
        PROTOT=PROTOT-TIE*(YHSD(9)-YHSD(5))                              774
        THE=(PROTOT-ACTTOT)/(YHSD(8)-YHSD(5))                            775
        HSDN(5)=HSDN(5)+THE                                              776
        HSDN(8)=HSDN(8)-THE                                              777
  105   HSDN(5)=HSDN(5)+TIE                                              778
        HSDN(9)=HSDN(9)-TIE                                             779
        WRITE(NO,110)(ARRAY(I),I=5,9),(HSDN(I),I=5,9)                    780
  110   FORMAT(28H NEW URBAN HOUSEHOLD NUMBERS/5(3X,A1,3X)/5F7.1/)       781
        RETURN                                                          782
        END                                                             783
                                                                        784

        SUBROUTINE JOBS(EMPLOY)
C THIS SUBROUTINE CALCULATES NUMBERS IN WAGE EMPLOYMENT IN EACH INCOME    786
C CLASS AND THUS NUMBERS NOT IN WAGE EMPLOYMENT                          787
        REAL JOBNOS                                                     788
        DIMENSION ARRAY(9),SECTOR(10),GO(10),GROW(10)
        DIMENSION RIO(10,10), WP(9,10), WG(9,10), RN(9,10)
        DIMENSION DEPR(10), RITX(10), RINT(10), RIMP(10), RIMT(10)
        DIMENSION CONV(10,5), HSDN(9), YHSD(9), TAXS(9), SAVG(9)
        DIMENSION CONS(10,4), TRAF(9,4), RIMD(9), RDUT(9)
        DIMENSION RIMC(10), CAPF(10), COSV(10), CAPUT(10)
        DIMENSION PIMP(10), PWAG(10), PREN(10), PDEP(10), PINT(10)
        DIMENSION PTAX(10), CAPAC(10)
        DIMENSION CONST(10), FD(10), WAGES(9), RENTS(9), FACINF(9),YOLD(9)
        DIMENSION CONSIM(10), CONDEM(10), PRICE(10), SUBS(10), TOTCOV(9)
        DIMENSION EMPLOY(9,10)
        DIMENSION BASEGO(10)
        DIMENSION GOLD(10)
        DIMENSION REXP(10), RINV(10), STOC(10)
        DIMENSION JOBNOS(9,10), TOTWAG(9), TOTNOT(9)
        COMMON/BLOCK1/ARRAY,SECTOR,GO,NYEAR,NI,NO,NBASE
        COMMON/BLOCK2/RIO,WP,WG,RN,DEPR,RITX,RINT,RIMP,RIMT              017
        COMMON/BLOCK3/CONV,HSDN,YHSD,TAXS,SAVG,CONS,TRAF,RIMD,RDUT       018
        COMMON/BLOCK4/RIMC,CAPF,COSV,CAPUT
        COMMON/BLOCK5/PIMP,PWAG,PREN,PDEP,PINT,PTAX                      020
C CALCULATE WAGE EMPLOYMENT AS A FUNCTION OF GROSS OUTPUT PER SECTOR     792
        DO 20 I=1,9                                                     793
        DO 10 J=1,10
```

```
            JOBNOS(I,J)=EMPLOY(I,J)*GO(J)                                    795
   10    CONTINUE                                                             796
   20    CONTINUE                                                             797
C  WRITE OUT MATRIX OF WAGE EMPLOYMENT                                        798
         WRITE(NO,30)NYEAR,ARRAY
   30    FORMAT( 11H MATRIX OF ,I4,16H WAGE EMPLOYMENT//19X,9(6X,A1)/)        800
         DO 40 I=1,10
         WRITE(NO,50)SECTOR(I).(JOBNOS(J,I),J=1,9)                           802
   40    CONTINUE                                                            803
   50    FORMAT(14X,A6,9F7.1)                                                804
C  CALCULATE TOTALS OF WAGE EMPLOYED AND NOT WAGE EMPLOYED                   805
         DO 70 I=1,9                                                         806
         TOTWAG(I)=0                                                         807
         DO 60 J=1,10
         TOTWAG(I)=TOTWAG(I)+JOBNOS(I,J)                                     809
   60    CONTINUE                                                            810
         TOTNOT(I)=HSDN(I)-TOTWAG(I)                                         811
   70    CONTINUE                                                            812
         DO 75 I=6,8                                                         813
         IF(TOTNOT(I).GE.10.0)GO TO 75                                       814
         TOTWAG(5)=TOTWAG(5)+10.0-TOTNOT(I)                                  815
         TOTNOT(5)=HSDN(5)-TOTWAG(5)                                        816
         TOTNOT(I)=10.0                                                      817
         TOTWAG(I)=HSDN(I)-TOTNOT(I)                                         818
   75    CONTINUE                                                            819
         IF(TOTNOT(4).GE.1.0)GO TO 78                                        820
         TOTWAG(1)=TOTWAG(1)+1.0-TOTNOT(4)                                   821
         TOTNOT(1)=HSDN(1)-TOTWAG(1)                                         822
         TOTNOT(4)=1.0                                                       823
         TOTWAG(4)=HSDN(4)-TOTNOT(4)                                         824
   78    CONTINUE                                                            825
         WRITE(NO,80)TOTWAG                                                  826
   80    FORMAT(/20H TOTAL WAGE EMPLOYED,9F7.1)                              827
C  FOR THE ZIMBABWE MODEL, CALCULATING TOTAL NOT WAGE EMPLOYED DOES
C  NOT MAKE SENSE - HENCE BYPASS THIS OUTPUT
         GO TO 9.9
         WRITE(NO,90)TOTNOT                                                  828
   90    FORMAT(/20H TOTAL NOT WAGE EMP.,9F7.1)                              829
  999    CONTINUE
         WRITE(NO,100)HSDN                                                   830
  100    FORMAT(/20H TOTAL NO HOUSEHOLDS,9F7.1/)                             831
         RETURN                                                             832
         END                                                                833
```

```
      SUBROUTINE DEMAND(CONDEM,CONDUT,CONSAV,CONTAX)                    834
C THIS SUBROUTINE CALCULATES TOTAL DEMAND FOR THE 4 DIRECT CONSUMPTION  835
C SECTORS AND CONVERTS THIS TO 9 SECTOR DEMAND.IT ALSO COMPUTES TOTAL   836
C CONSUMER TAXES,SAVINGS AND DIRECT IMPORTS                             837
      DIMENSION ARRAY(9),SECTOR(10),GO(10),GROW(10)
      DIMENSION RIO(10), WP(9,10), WG(9,10), RN(9,10)
      DIMENSION DEPR(10), RITX(10), RINT(10), RIMP(10), RIMT(10)
      DIMENSION CONV(10,5), HSDN(9), YHSD(9), TAXS(9), SAVG(9)
      DIMENSION CONS(10,4), TRAF(9,4), RIMD(9), RDUT(9)
      DIMENSION RIMC(10), CAPF(10), COSV(10), CAPUT(10)
      DIMENSION PIMP(10), PWAG(10), PREN(10), PDEP(10), PINT(10)
      DIMENSION PTAX(10), CAPAC(10)
      DIMENSION CONST(10), FD(10), WAGES(9), RENTS(9), FACINF(9),YOLD(9)
      DIMENSION CONSIM(10), CONDEM(10), PRICE(10), SUBS(10,, TOTCOV(9)
      DIMENSION EMPLOY(9,10)
      DIMENSION BASEGO(10)
      DIMENSION GOLD(10)
      DIMENSION REXP(10), RINV(10), STOC(10)                            017
      DIMENSION DCON(4)                                                 018
      COMMON/BLOCK1/ARRAY,SECTOR,GO,NYEAR,NI,NO,NBASE                   020
      COMMON/BLOCK2/RIO,WP,WG,RN,DEPR,RITX,RINT,RIMP,RIMT               844
      COMMON/BLOCK3/CONV,HSDN,YHSD,TAXS,SAVG,CONS,TRAF,RIMC,RDUT        845
      COMMON/BLOCK4/RIMC,CAPF,COSV,CAPUT                                846
      COMMON/BLOCK5/PIMP,PWAG,PREN,PDEP,PINT,PTAX                       847
C CALCULATE TOTAL CONSUMER DEMAND FOR THE 4 DIRECT CONSUMPTION SECTORS  848
      DO 20 I=1,4                                                       849
      DCON(I)=0                                                         850
      DO 10 J=1,9                                                       851
   10 DCON(I)=DCON(I)+YHSD(J)*HSDN(J)*CONS(J,I)                         852
   20 CONTINUE
   25 FORMAT(/26H DIRECT CONSUMPTION DEMAND/4(3X,A6)/4F9.0/)
      WRITE(NO,25)SECTOR(1),SECTOR(5),SECTOR(6),SECTOR(8),DCON
C CONVERT DEMAND ON 4 DIRECT CONSUMPTION SECTORS TO 10 SECTOR DEMAND
      DO 40 I=1,10                                                      855
      CONDEM(I)=0                                                       856
      DO 30 J=1,4                                                       857
      CONDEM(I)=CONDEM(I)+CONV(I,J)*DCON(J)                             858
   30 CONTINUE                                                          859
   40 CONTINUE                                                          860
      WRITE(NO,50)NYEAR,SECTOR,CONDEM
   50 FORMAT(I5,30H CONSUMER DEMAND ON 10 SECTORS/10(3X,A6)/10F9.0/)
```

164

```
C  CONSTRAIN DEMAND ON MODAG AND ADD TO TRAD
      CALL AGCON(CONDEM)                                              863
      CONDUT=0                                                        864
      CONTAX=0                                                        865
      CONSAV=0                                                        866
C  COMPUTE TOTAL TAXES,SAVINGS,DIRECT CONSUMER IMPORTS AND DUTY       867
      CONIMP=0                                                        868
      DO 60 I=1,9                                                     869
      CONTAX=CONTAX+YHSD(I)*HSDN(I)*TAXS(I)                           870
      CONSAV=CONSAV+YHSD(I)*HSDN(I)*SAVG(I)                           871
      CONIMP=CONIMP+YHSD(I)*HSDN(I)*RIMD(I)                           872
      CONDUT=CONDUT+YHSD(I)*HSDN(I)*RIMD(I)*RDUT(I)                   873
   60 CONTINUE                                                        874
      WRITE(NO,70)NYEAR,CONTAX                                        875
   70 FORMAT(42H TOTAL CONSUMER TAXES AVAILABLE FOR USE IN,I5,2H =,F9.0)  876
      WRITE(NO,80)NYEAR,CONSAV                                        877
   80 FORMAT(42H TOTAL CONSUM SAVINGS AVAILABLE FOR USE IN,I5,2H =,F9.0)  878
      K=NYEAR-1                                                       879
      WRITE(NO,90)K,CONIMP,CONDUT                                     880
   90 FORMAT(30H TOTAL DIRECT CONSUMER IMPORTS,I5,2H =,F9.0,          881
     17H DUTY =,F9.0)                                                 882
      RETURN
      END

      SUBROUTINE GOVERN(CONDEM,SUBS,CAPIMD,TOTITX,TOTIMD,CONDUT,      884
     1CONTAX)                                                         885
C  THIS SUBROUTINE COMPUTES GOVERNMENT INCOME AS THE SUM OF TAXES,DUTY  886
C  AND LOANS.GOVERNMENT EXPENDITURE IS READ IN AND DEFICIT=EXP-INCOME.  887
C  THE SUBROUTINE ALSO CALCULATES THE FINAL DEMAND ON THE GOVT SECTOR
      DIMENSION ARRAY(9),SECTOR(10),GO(10),GRQW(10)
      DIMENSION RIO(10,10), WP(9,10), WG(9,10), RN(9,10)
      DIMENSION DEPR(10), RITX(10), RINT(10), RIMP(10), RIMT(10)
      DIMENSION CONV(10,5), HSDN(9), YHSD(9), TAXS(9), SAVG(9)
      DIMENSION CONS(10,4), TRAF(9,4), RIMD(9), RDUT(9)
      DIMENSION RIMC(10), CAPF(10), COSV(10), CAPUT(10)
      DIMENSION PIMP(10), PWAG(10), PREN(10), PDEP(10), PINT(10)
      DIMENSION PTAX(10), CAPAC(10)
      DIMENSION CONST(10), FD(10), WAGES(9), RENTS(9), FACINF(9),YOLD(9)
      DIMENSION CONSIM(10), CONDEM(10), PRICE(10), SUBS(10), TOTCOV(9)
      DIMENSION EMPLOY(9,10)
      DIMENSION BASEGO(10)
      DIMENSION GOLD(10)
```

165

```
      DIMENSION REXP(10), RINV(10), STOC(10)                                    017
      COMMON/BLOCK1/ARRAY,SECTOR,GD,NYEAR,NI,NO,NBASE
      COMMON/BLOCK2/RIO,WP,WG,RN,DEPR,RITX,RINT,RIMP,RIMT
      COMMON/BLOCK3/CONV,HSDN,YHSD,TAXS,SAVG,CONS,TRAF,RIMD.RDUT
      COMMON/BLOCK4/RIMC,CAPF,COSV,CAPUT                                        018
      COMMON/BLOCK5/PIMP,PWAG,PREN,PDEP,PINT,PTAX
C  CALCULATE TOTAL OF INDIRECT TAXES+DIRECT TAXES +DUTY FROM EARLIER SUBR       020
      GOVINC=TOTITX+CONTAX+TOTIMD+CAPIMD+CONDUT                                 891
      WRITE(NO,10)GOVINC                                                        892
   10 FORMAT(58H GOVERNMENT INCOME FROM INDIRECT TAXES+DIRECT TAXES+DUTY        893
     1 =,F9.0/)                                                                 894
C  READ LOANS(INTERNAL AND EXTERNAL)AND LOAN SERVICE ADD LOANS TO GOV INC       895
      READ(NI,20)GOVL,GOVLS                                                     896
   20 FORMAT(10X,F6.0,2X,F6.0)                                                  897
      GOVINC=GOVINC+GOVL                                                        898
      WRITE(NO,30)GOVINC                                                        899
   30 FORMAT(26H TOTAL GOVERNMENT INCOME =,F9.0/)                               900
C  READ IN GOVERNMENT POLICY ON CONSUMPTION EXPENDITURE,CAPITAL FORMATION       901
C  AND SUBSIDIES-CALCULATE TOTAL GOVERNMENT EXPENDITURE                         902
      READ(NI,40)GOVCON,GOVCAP,SUBS(2)                                          903
   40 FORMAT(22X,F8.0,10X F8.0,4X F6.0)                                         904
      GOVEXP=GOVCON+GOVCAP+SUBS(2)+GOVLS                                        905
      WRITE(NO,50)GOVEXP                                                        906
   50 FORMAT(31H TOTAL GOVERNMENT EXPENDITURE =,F9.0/)                          907
C  CALCULATE DEFICIT OR SURPLUS                                                 908
      DEF=GOVEXP-GOVINC                                                         909
      IF(DEF.LT.0)GO TO 70                                                      910
      WRITE(NO,60)DEF                                                           911
   60 FORMAT(21H GOVERNMENT DEFICIT =,F7.0/)                                    912
      GO TO 90
   70 SURP=-DEF                                                                 914
      WRITE(NO,80)SURP                                                          915
   80 FORMAT(21H GOVERNMENT SURPLUS =,F7.0/)                                    916
C  SET UP FINAL DEMAND ON GOVERNMENT SECTOR
   90 CONDEM(9)=CONDEM(9)+GOVCON                                                918
      WRITE(NO,100)CONDEM(9)                                                    919
  100 FORMAT(41H CONSUMPTION DEMAND ON GOVERNMENT SECTOR=,F9.0/)                920
      RETURN                                                                    921
      END                                                                       922
                                                                               923

      SUBROUTINE CAPFORM(CONSAV)                                                925
C  THIS SUBROUTINE CALCULATES CAPITAL FORMATION AS THE SUM OF CONSUMER
```

```
C     SAVINGS,BUSINESS SAVINGS,GOVERMENT CAPITAL EXPENDITURE AND PRIVATE    926
C     CAPITAL IMPORTS                                                       927
      DIMENSION ARRAY(9),SECTOR(10),GO(10),GROW(10)
      DIMENSION RIO(10,10), WP(9,10), WG(9,10), RN(9,10)
      DIMENSION DEPR(10), RITX(10), RINT(10), RIMP(10), RIMT(10)
      DIMENSION CONV(10,5), HSDN(9), YHSD(9), TAXS(9), SAVG(9)
      DIMENSION CONS(10,4), TRAF(9,4), RIMD(9), RDUT(9)
      DIMENSION RIMC(10), CAPF(10), COSV(10), CAPUT(:0)
      DIMENSION PIMP(10), PWAG(10), PREN(10), PDEP(10), PINT(10)
      DIMENSION PTAX(10), CAPAC(10)
      DIMENSION CONST(10), FD(10), WAGES(9), RENTS(9), FACINF(9),YOLD(9)
      DIMENSION CONSIM(10), CONDEM(10), PRICE(10), SUBS(1C), TOTCOV(9)
      DIMENSION EMPLOY(9,10)
      DIMENSION BASEGO(10)
      DIMENSION GOLD(10)
      DIMENSION REXP(10), RINV(10), STOC(10)
      DIMENSION DEP(10), SAVCON(10),GOVI(10), PRIVI(10)
      COMMON/BLOCK1/ARRAY,SECTOR,GO,NYEAR,NI,NO,NBASE
      COMMON/BLOCK2/RIO,WP,WG,RN,DEPR,RITX,RINT,RIMP,RIMT              017
      COMMON/BLOCK3/CONV,HSDN,YHSD,TAXS,SAVG,CONS,TRAF,RIMC,RDUT       018
      COMMON/BLOCK4/RIMC,CAPF,COSV,CAPUT
      COMMON/BLOCK5/PIMP,PWAG,PREN,PDEP,PINT,PTAX                      020
C     READ IN GOVERNMENT INVESTMENT AND IMPORTED PRIVATE CAPITAL INVESTMENT 933
C     IN 10 SECTORS
      CALL READV3(GOVI)
      CALL READV3(PRIVI)
      WRITE(NO,20)SECTOR,GOVI,PRIVI                                    937
   20 FORMAT(28H CAPITAL FORMATION BY SECTOR/12X,10A6/11H GOVERNMENT,2X,  9
     110F6.0/13H IMPT PRIVATE,10F6.0)
C     CALCULATE DEPRECIATION PER SECTOR                                940
      DO 30 I=1,10
      DEP(I)=GO(I)*DEPR(I)
   30 CONTINUE
      WRITE(NO,40)DEP                                                  942
   40 FORMAT(13H DEPRECIATION,10F6.0)                                  943
C     CALCULATE ALLOCATION OF CONSUMER SAVINGS BETWEEN SECTORS         944
      DO 50 I=1,10
      SAVCON(I)=CONSAV*COSV(I)                                         946
   50 CONTINUE
      WRITE(NO,60)SAVCON                                               948
   60 FORMAT(13H CONS SAVINGS,10F6.0)                                  949
C     CALCULATE TOTAL CAPITAL FORMATION FOR 10 SECRORS                 950
```

167

```
        DO 70 I=1,10
        CAPF(I)=GOVI(I)+PRIVI(I)+DEP(I)+SAVCON(I)          954
 70     CONTINUE                                           955
        WRITE(NO,80)CAPF                                   95?
 80     FORMAT(/13H TOT CAP FORM,10F6.0/)                  958
        RETURN                                             959
        END

        SUBROUTINE CONSTEF(CONST)
C  THIS SUBROUTINE DETERMINES THE DEMAND ON THE 10 SECTORS GENERATED BY
C  THE CONSTRUCTION EFFECT OF CAPITAL INVESTMENT           962
        DIMENSION ARRAY(9),SECTOR(10),GO(10),GROW(10)
        DIMENSION RIO(10,10), WP(9,10), WG(9,10), RN(9,10)
        DIMENSION DEPR(10), RITX(10), RINT(10), RIMP(10), RINT(10)
        DIMENSION CONV(10,5), HSDN(9), YHSD(9), TAXS(9), SAVC(9)
        DIMENSION CONS(10,4), TRAF(9,4), RIMD(9), ROUT(9)
        DIMENSION RIMC(10), CAPF(10), COSV(10), CAPUT(10)
        DIMENSION PIMP(10), PwAG(10), PREN(10), PDEP(10), PINT(10)
        DIMENSION PTAX(10), CAPAC(10)
        DIMENSION CONST(10), FD(10), WAGES(9), RENTS(9), FACINF(9),YOLD(9)
        DIMENSION CONSIM(10), CONDEM(10), PRICE(10), SUBS(10), TOTCOV(9)
        DIMENSION EMPLOY(9,10)
        DIMENSION BASEGO(10)
        DIMENSION GOLD(10)
        DIMENSION REXP(10), RINV(10), STOC(10)
        DIMENSION CAPIM(10), REMCAP(10), BANDC(10), SERV(10)
        COMMON/BLOCK1/ARRAY,SECTOR,GO,NYEAR,NI,NO,NBASE
        COMMON/BLOCK2/RIO,WP,WG,RN,DEPR,RITX,RINT,RIMP,RIMT
        COMMON/BLOCK3/CONV,HSDN,YHSD,TAXS,SAVG,CONS,TRAF,RIMD,ROUT
        COMMON/BLOCK4/RIMC,CAPF,COSV,CAPUT
        COMMON/BLOCK5/PIMP,PWAG,PREN,PDEP,PINT,PTAX
C  SUBTRACT FROM CAPITAL INVESTED PER SECTOR THE AMOUNT SPENT ON CAPITAL
C  IMPORTS                                                 966
        DO 10 I=1,10                                       967
        CAPIM(I)=CAPF(I)*RIMC(I)                           969
        REMCAP(I)=CAPF(I)-CAPIM(I)                         970
 10     CONTINUE                                           971
C  READ IN THE PROPORTION OF THE REMAINING INVESTMENT PER SECTOR WHICH   017
C  RESULTS IN A CONSTRUCTION EFFECT DEMAND ON B+C AND SERVICES           018
        CALL READV7(BANDC)                                 972
        CALL READV7(SERV)                                  973
        DO 30 I=1,10
```

168

```
        BANDC(I)=REMCAP(I)*BANDC(I)                                          977
        SERV(I)=REMCAP(I)*SERV(I)                                            978
        REMCAP(I)=REMCAP(I)-BANDC(I)-SERV(I)                                 979
 30     CONTINUE                                                             980
C  WRITE OUT THE SPLIT OF CAPITAL INVESTMENT BETWEEN CAPITAL IMPORTS AND      981
C  FINAL DEMAND ON BANDC,SERVICES AND OWN SECTOR                             982
        WRITE(NO,40)SECTOR                                                   983
 40     FORMAT(/42H CONSTRUCTION EFFECT OF CAPITAL INVESTMEN./21X,10A6)      985
        WRITE(NO,50)CAPIM
 50     FORMAT(16H CAPITAL IMPORTS,5X,10F6.0)                                987
        WRITE(NO,60)REMCAP
 60     FORMAT(21H DEMAND ON OWN SECTOR,10F6.0)                              989
        WRITE(NO,70)BANDC
 70     FORMAT(21H DEMAND ON B+C SECTOR,10F6.0)                              991
        WRITE(NO,80)SERV
 80     FORMAT(21H DEMAND ON SVC SECTOR,10F6.0,                              993
        WRITE(NO,90)CAPF
 90     FORMAT(10X,6H TOTAL,5X,10F6.0/)
C  CALCULATE THE CONSTRUCTION EFFECT FINAL DEMAND ON 10 SECTORS
        DO 100 I=1,10                                                        997
        CONST(I)=REMCAP(I)                                                   998
 100    CONTINUE
        DO 110 I=1,10                                                        1000
        CONST(4)=CONST(4)+BANDC(I)                                           1055
        CONST(8)=CONST(8)+SERV(I)                                            1056
 110    CONTINUE                                                             1057
        WRITE(NO,120)SECTOR,CONST
 120    FORMAT(33H CONSTRUCTION EFFECT FINAL DEMAND/1X,10A6/1X,10F6.0/)      1002
        RETURN                                                               1003
        END
        SUBROUTINE EXPORT(CONST,FD,CONDEM,SUBS)                              1004
C  THIS SUBROUTINE READS IN EXPORT AND STOCK CHANGE FIGURES AND COMPUTES      1005
C  FINAL DEMAND=CONSUMER DEMAND+ GOVT.CONS+CONST EFFECT+EXPORTS+STOCKS        1006
        DIMENSION ARRAY(9),SECTOR(10),GD(10),GROW(10)
        DIMENSION RIO(10,10),WP(9,10),WG(9,10),RN(9,10)
        DIMENSION DEPR(10),RITX(10),RINT(10),RIMP(10),RIMT(10)
        DIMENSION CONV(10,5),HSDN(9),YHSD(9),TAXS(9),SAVG(9)
        DIMENSION CONS(10,4),TRAF(9,4),RIMD(9),RDUT(9)
        DIMENSION RIMC(10),CAPF(10),COSV(10),CAPUT(10)
        DIMENSION PIMP(10),PWAG(10),PREN(10),PDEP(10),PJNT(10)
        DIMENSION PTAX(10),CAPAC(10)
```

169

```
      DIMENSION CONST(10), FD(10), WAGES(9), RENTS(9), FACTNF(9),YOLD(9)
      DIMENSION CONSIM(10), CONDEM(10), PRICE(10), SUBS(10), TOTCOV(9)
      DIMENSION EMPLOY(9,10)
      DIMENSION BASEGO(10)
      DIMENSION GOLD(10)
      DIMENSION REXP(10), RINV(10), STOC(10), EXPT(10), STOK(10)     017
      COMMON/BLOCK1/ARRAY,SECTOR,GO,NYEAR,NI,NO,NBASE                 018
      COMMON/BLOCK2/RIO,WP,WG,RN,DEPR,RITX,RINT,RIMP,RIMT
      COMMON/BLOCK3/CONV,HSDN,YHSD,TAXS,SAVG,CONS,TRAF,RIMC,RDUT
      COMMON/BLOCK4/RIMC,CAPF,COSV,CAPUT
      COMMON/BLOCK5/PIMP,PWAG,PREN,PDEP,PINT,PTAX                     020
C READ IN EXPORTS PER SECTOR                                         1010
      CALL READV2(EXPT)
C READ IN STOCK CHANGE PER SECTOR                                    1013
      CALL READV2(STOK)
      WRITE(NO,15)SECTOR,EXPT,STOK                                    1015
   15 FORMAT(/10X,10(4X,A6)/10H EXPORTS    ,10F10.0/10H STOCK CHA,10F10.0/
     1)                                                              1017
C CALCULATE FINAL DEMAND AS CONSUMER DEMAND+CONST EFFECT+EXPORTS+STOCKS
      DO 20 I=1,10                                                    1019
      FD(I)=CONDEM(I)+CONST(I)+EXPT(I)+STOK(I)                        1020
   20 CONTINUE                                                        1021
C MINOR AMENDMENT TO MODAG TO ADD IN SUBSIDIES                       1022
      FD(2)=FD(2)+SUBS(2)                                             1023
      WRITE(NO,30)NYEAR,SECTOR,FD
   30 FORMAT(I5,13H FINAL DEMAND/1X,10(1X,A6)/10(1X,F6.0)/)
      RETURN
      END

      SUBROUTINE PROD(FD,RIO)                                         1027
C THIS SUBROUTINE USES I/O ANALYSIS AND FINAL DEMAND DATA TO GENERATE 1028
C THE GROSS OUTPUT OF THE 10 PRODUCTINE SECTORS
      DIMENSION ARRAY(9),SECTOR(10),GO(10),RIO(10,10),A(1CO),FD(10),W(3)
      COMMON/BLOCK1/ARRAY,SECTOR,GO,NYEAR,NI,NO
C CALCULATE LHS MATRIX OF COEFFS FOR I/O ANALYSIS EQUATION
      DO 20 I=1,10                                                    1036
      DO 10 J=1,10                                                    1037
      K=I+10*(J-1)                                                    1038
      A(K)=-RIO(J,I)                                                  1039
      IF(I.EQ.J)A(K)=1+A(K)
   10 CONTINUE
   20 CONTINUE
```

170

```
C SOLVE SIMULTANEOUS EQUATIONS FOR GROSS OUTPUT OF 10 SECTORS AND PRINT
      M=10                                                              1043
      N=1                                                              1044
      E=.0000001
      CALL FPMGE(M,N,E,A(1),FD(1),W(1),DET,IRANK,NRR)
      DO 30 I=1,10                                                      1047
      GO(I)=FD(I)                                                       1048
   30 CONTINUE                                                          1049
      WRITE(NO,40)NYEAR,SECTOR,GO
   40 FORMAT(/I5,25H PROVISIONAL GROSS OUTPUT/10(2X,A6,2X)/10F10.0//)    1051
      RETURN                                                            1052
      END

      SUBROUTINE CAPCTY(CONSIM,CAPAC,GROW,GOLD)
C THIS SUBROUTINE CHECKS IF THE PROVISIONAL GROSS OUTPUT OF EACH SECTOR  1054
C IS WITHIN THE CAPACITY CONSTRAINT.IF NOT,THE BALANCE IS IMPORTED.      1058
C IN THE CASE OF MODERN AGRICULTURE A WEATHER FACTOR IS ALSO CONSIDERED  1059
      DIMENSION ARRAY(9),SECTOR(10),GO(10),GROW(10)
      DIMENSION RIO(10,10), WP(9,10), WG(9,10), RN(9,10)
      DIMENSION DEPR(10), RITX(10), RINT(10), RIMP(10), RIMT(10)
      DIMENSION CONV(10,5), HSDN(9), YHSD(9), TAXS(9), SAVG(9)
      DIMENSION CONS(10,4), TRAF(9,4), RIMD(9), RDUT(9)
      DIMENSION RIMC(10), CAPF(10), COSV(10), CAPUT(10)
      DIMENSION PIMP(10), PWAG(10), PREN(10), PDEP(10), PINT(10)
      DIMENSION PTAX(10), CAPAC(10)
      DIMENSION CONST(10), FD(10), WAGES(9), RENTS(9), FACINF(9),YOLD(9)
      DIMENSION CONSIM(10), CONDEM(10), PRICE(10), SUBS(10), TOTCOV(9)
      DIMENSION EMPLOY(9,10)
      DIMENSION BASEGO(10)
      DIMENSION GOLD(10)
      DIMENSION REXP(10),    RINV(10), STOC(10)
      DIMENSION ANNGR(10)
      COMMON/BLOCK1/ARRAY,SECTOR,GO,NYEAR,NI,NO,NBASE
      COMMON/BLOCK2/RIO,WP,WG,RN,DEPR,RITX,RINT,RIMP,RIMT                017
      COMMON/BLOCK3/CONV,HSDN,YHSD,TAXS,SAVG,CONS,TRAF,RIMD,RDUT         018
      COMMON/BLOCK4/RIMC,CAPF,COSV,CAPUT
      COMMON/BLOCK5/PIMP,PWAG,PREN,PDEP,PINT,PTAX
C READ IN THE WEATHER FACTOR FOR MODERN AGRICULTURE AND AMEND THE CAPAC.
      READ(NI,5)AGWTTR,AGWTAG                                           020
    5 FORMAT(10X,F6.3,2X,F6.3)                                          1064
      CAPAC(1)=CAPAC(1)*AGWTTR
      CAPAC(2)=CAPAC(2)*AGWTAG
```

171

```fortran
      DO 30 I=1,10
C CHECK IF PROVISIONAL GROSS OUTPUT IS LESS THAN OR EQUAL TO CAPACITY    1069
      IF(GO(I).LE.CAPAC(I))GO TO 20                                      1070
      CONSIM(I)=GO(I)-CAPAC(I)                                           1071
      GO(I)=GO(I)-CONSIM(I)                                             1072
      GO TO 30                                                          1073
   20 CONSIM(I)=0                                                       1074
   30 CONTINUE                                                          1075
      GOOLD=0                                                           1076
      GONEW=0                                                           1077
      DO 35 I=1,10
      GOOLD=GOOLD+GOLD(I)                                                1079
      GONEW=GONEW+GO(I)                                                  1080
      ANNGR(I)=GO(I)/GOLD(I)                                             1081
      GROW(I)=GROW(I)*ANNGR(I)                                           1082
      GOLD(I)=GO(I)                                                      1083
   35 CONTINUE                                                           1084
      TOTGR=GONEW/GOOLD                                                  1085
      WRITE(NO,40)NYEAR                                                  1086
   40 FORMAT(/I5,51H FINAL OUTPUT OF EACH SECTOR AND CONSUMPTION IMPORT)  1087
      WRITE(NO,50)SECTOR,GO,GONEW,CONSIM,ANNGR,TOTGR                     1088
   50 FORMAT(10(2X,A6,2X),4X,6H TOTAL/11F10.0/10F10.0/3H GR,11(F7.3,3X))
      RETURN                                                            1090
      END                                                               1091

      SUBROUTINE FPMGE(M,N,E,A,B,W,DET,IRANK,NRR)
      DIMENSION A(10,10),B(10),X(10),DIGITS(10),SCRA(10,15)
C MAKE A CALL TO SUBROUTINS LINQZ
      CALL LINQZ(M,10,1,A,B,X,DET,DIGITS,SCRA,NRR)
      DO 1 I=1,10
    1 B(I)=X(I)
      RETURN
      END
```

#LINQZ is a matrix inversion routine.

```fortran
      SUBROUTINE RATE(BASEGO,GROW,NEND)
C THIS SUBROUTINE CALCULATES THE OVERALL GROWTHRATE OF THE ECONOMY
      DIMENSION ARRAY(9), SECTOR(10), GO(10)
      DIMENSION BASEGO(10), GROW(10)
      COMMON/BLOCK1/ARRAY,SECTOR,GO,NYEAR,NI,NO,NBASE
      TOTBAS=0
```

172

```
      TOTEND=0                                                          110
      DO 120 I=1,10
      TOTBAS=TOTBAS+BASEGO(I)
      TOTEND=TOTEND+BASEGO(I)*GROW(I)
  120 CONTINUE
      TOTGR=TOTEND/TOTBAS                                               112
      NOYR=NYEAR-NBASE                                                  113
      POWER=1.0/NOYR                                                    114
      RAT =(TOTGR**POWER-1)*100.                                        115
      WRITE(NO,130)RAT, NBASE,NEND
  130 FORMAT(34H OVERALL GROWTH RATE OF ECONOMY = ,F6.2,12HPC PER ANNUM, 117
     11X, 5HFROM ,I4,9H THROUGH ,I4)
      RETURN
      END

      SUBROUTINE READM(RMAT)                                           280
C THIS SUBROUTINE READS IN A 9X10INPUT MATRIX.TOGETHER WITH DESCRIPTION
C AND WRITES IT OUT
      DIMENSION ARRAY(9),SECTOR(10),GO(10),GROW(10)                     282
      DIMENSION RMAT(9,10), ARR(10)
      COMMON/BLOCK1/ARRAY,SECTOR,GO,NYEAR,NI,NO,NBASE
      INTEGER SCALE
      DO 10 I=1,10
      READ(NI,20)DESC,SCALE,(ARR(J),RMAT(J,I),J=1,9)                    285
      SUM=0.
      DO 5 J=1,9
      SUM=SUM+RMAT(J,I)
    5 CONTINUE
      WRITE(NO,30)DESC,(ARR(J),RMAT(J,I),J=1,9),SUM,SCALE               286
   10 CONTINUE                                                          287
   20 FORMAT(A7,I1,9(A2,F6.0))                                          288
   30 FORMAT(1X,A7,1H ,9(A2,F6.0),8X,F10.0,* DATA IN E*,I2,* SCALE*)
      RETURN
      END

      SUBROUTINE READM1(RMAT)
C THIS SUBROUTINE READS IN A10X10INPUT MATRIX.TOGETHER WITH DESCRIPTION
C AND WRITES IT OUT
      DIMENSION ARRAY(9),SECTOR(10),GO(10),GROW(10)
      DIMENSION RMAT(10,10), ARR(10),DESC(10)
      COMMON/BLOCK1/ARRAY,SECTOR,GO,NYEAR,NI,NO,NBASE
      INTEGER SCALE
```

173

```
          DO 10 I=1,10
          READ(NI,20)DESC(I),SCALE,(ARR(J),RMAT(J,I),J=1,9)
          READ(NI,21)ADESC,SCALE,ARR(10),RMAT(10,I)
   10     CONTINUE
          DO 40 I=1,10
          DO 5 J=1,10
          SUM=SUM+RMAT(J,I)
   5      CONTINUE
   40     CONTINUE
          WRITE(NO,30)DESC(I),(ARR(J),RMAT(J,I),J=1,10),SUM,SCALE
   20 FORMAT(A7,I1, 9(A2,F6.0))
   21 FORMAT(A7,I1,A2,F6.0)
   30 FORMAT(1X,A7,1H ,10(A2,F6.0),F10.0,* DATA IN E*,I2,* SCALE*)
          RETURN
          END

      SUBROUTINE READVC(RVEC)                                            293
C THIS SUBROUTINE READS IN A 9X1 INPUT VECTOR TOGETHER WITH DESCRIPTION
C SUMSIT AND WRITES IT OUT
      DIMENSION ARRAY(9),SECTOR(10),GO(10),GROW(10)                      295
      DIMENSION RVEC(9),ARR(9)
      COMMON/BLOCK1/ARRAY,SECTOR,GO,NYEAR,NI,NO,NBASE
      INTEGER SCALE
      SUM=0.
      SUM=0.
          READ(NI,10)DESC,SCALE,(ARR(I),RVEC(I),I=1,9)
   10 FORMAT(A7,I1,9(A2,F6.0))
          DO 5 J=1,9
          SUM=SUM RVEC(J)
   5      CONTINUE
          WRITE(NO,20)DESC,(ARR(I),RVEC(I),I=1,9),SUM ,SCALE             298
   20 FORMAT(1X,A7,1H ,9(A2,F6.0),8X,F10.0,* DATA IN E*,I2,* SCALE*)     301
          RETURN                                                         302
          END

      SUBROUTINE READV1(RVEC)                                            293
C THIS SUBROUTINE READS IN A 9X1 INPUT VECTOR TOGETHER WITH DESCRIPTION  294
C AND WRITES IT OUT
      DIMENSION ARRAY(9),SECTOR(10),GO(10),GROW(10)
      DIMENSION RVEC(9),ARR(9)
      COMMON/BLOCK1/ARRAY,SECTOR,GO,NYEAR,NI,NO,NBASE
      INTEGER SCALE
```

```
   10 READ(NI,10)DESC,SCALE,(ARR(I),RVEC(I),I=1,9)
      FORMAT(A7,I1,9(A2,F6.3))
   20 WRITE(NO,20)DESC,(ARR(I),RVEC(I),I=1,9),SCALE
      FORMAT(1X,A7,1H ,9(A2,F6.3),18X,     DATA IN E*,I2,* SCALE*)
      RETURN
      END

      SUBROUTINE READV2(RVEC)
C THIS SUBROUTINE READS IN A 10X1 INPUT VECTOR TOGETHER WITH DESCRIPTION
C AND WRITES IT OUT
      DIMENSION ARRAY(9),SECTOR(10),GO(10),GROW(10)
      DIMENSION RVEC(10), ARR(10)
      COMMON/BLOCK1/ARRAY,SECTOR,GO,NYEAR,N1,NO,NBASE
      INTEGER SCALE
      READ(NI,10)DESC,SCALE,(ARR(I),RVEC(I),I=1,9)
      READ(NI,11)ADESC,SCALE,ARR(10),RVEC(10)
   10 FORMAT(A7,I1, 9(A2,F6.0))
   11 FORMAT(A7,I1,A2,F6.0)
   20 WRITE(NO,20)DESC,(ARR(I),RVEC(I),I=1,10),SCALE
      FORMAT(1X,A7,1H ,10(A2,F6.0), * DATA IN E*,I2,* SCALE*)
      RETURN
      END

      SUBROUTINE READV3(RVEC)
C THIS SUBROUTINE READS IN A 10X1 INPUT VECTOR TOGETHER WITH DESCRIPTION
C AND WRITES IT OUT AFTER SUMMING
      DIMENSION ARRAY(9),SECTOR(10),GO(10),GROW(10)
      DIMENSION RVEC(10), ARR(10)
      COMMON/BLOCK1/ARRAY,SECTOR,GO,NYEAR,NI,NO,NBASE
      INTEGER SCALE
      SUM=0.
      READ(NI,10)DESC,SCALE,(ARR(I),RVEC(I),I=1,9)
      READ(NI,11)ADESC,SCALE,ARR(10),RVEC(10)
   10 FORMAT(A7,I1, 9(A2,F6.0))
   11 FORMAT(A7,I1,A2,F6.0)
      DO 5 J=1,10
      SUM=SUM+RVEC(J)
    5 CONTINUE
   20 WRITE(NO,20)DESC,(ARR(I),RVEC(I),I=1,10),SUM ,SCALE
      FORMAT(1X,A7,1H ,10(A2,F6.0),F10.0,* DATA IN E*,I2,* SCALE*)
      RETURN
      END
```

175

```
      SUBROUTINE READV4(RVEC)
C THIS SUBROUTINE READS IN A 10X1 INPUT VECTOR TOGETHER WITH DESCRIPTION
C AND WRITES IT OUT - USING F6.2
      DIMENSION ARRAY(9),SECTOR(10),GO(10),GROW(10)
      DIMENSION RVEC(10), ARR(10)
      COMMON/BLOCK1/ARRAY,SECTOR,GO,NYEAR,NI,NO,NBASE
      INTEGER SCALE
      READ(NI,10)DESC,SCALE,(ARR(I),RVEC(I),I=1,9)
      READ(NI,11)ADESC,SCALE,ARR(10),RVEC(10)
   10 FORMAT(A7,I1, 9(A2,F6.2))
   11 FORMAT(A7,I1,A2,F6.2)
      WRITE(NO,20)DESC,(ARR(I),RVEC(I),I=1,10),SCALE
   20 FORMAT(1X,A7,1H ,10(A2,F6.2), * DATA IN E*,I2,* SCALE*)
      RETURN
      END

      SUBROUTINE READV5(RVEC)
C THIS SUBROUTINE READS IN A 10X1 INPUT VECTOR TOGETHER WITH DESCRIPTION
C AND WRITES IT OUT - USING F6.3
      DIMENSION ARRAY(9),SECTOR(10),GO(10),GROW(10)
      DIMENSION RVEC(10), ARR(10)
      COMMON/BLOCK1/ARRAY,SECTOR,GO,NYEAR,NI,NO,NBASE
      INTEGER SCALE
      READ(NI,10)DESC,      (ARR(I),RVEC(I),I=1,9)
      READ(NI,11)ADESC,      ARR(10),RVEC(10)
   10 FORMAT(A7,1X, 9(A2,F6.4))
   11 FORMAT(A7,1X,A2,F6.4)
      WRITE(NO,20)DESC,(ARR(I),RVEC(I),I=1,10),SCALE
   20 FORMAT(1X,A7,1H ,10(A2,F6.3), * DATA IN E*,I2,* SCALE*)
      RETURN
      END

      SUBROUTINE READV6(RVEC)
C THIS SUBROUTINE READS IN A 10X1 INPUT VECTOR TOGETHER WITH DESCRIPTION
C - USING F6.4
      DIMENSION ARRAY(9),SECTOR(10),GO(10),GROW(10)
      DIMENSION RVEC(10), ARR(10)
      COMMON/BLOCK1/ARRAY,SECTOR,GO,NYEAR,NI,NO,NBASE
      INTEGER SCALE
      READ(NI,10)DESC,      (ARR(I),RVEC(I),I=1,9)
      READ(NI,11)ADESC,      ARR(10),RVEC(10)
```

176

```
   10 FORMAT(A7,1X, 9(A2,F6.4))
   11 FORMAT(A7,1X,A2,F6.4)
      RETURN
      END

      SUBROUTINE READV7(RVEC)
C THIS SUBROUTINE READS IN A 10X1 INPUT VECTOR TOGETHER WITH DESCRIPTION
C AND WRITES IT OUT - USING F6.4
      DIMENSION ARRAY(9),SECTOR(10),GO(10),GROW(10)
      DIMENSION RVEC(10), ARR(10)
      COMMON/BLOCK1/ARRAY,SECTOR,GO,NYEAR,NI,NO,NBASE
      INTEGER SCALE
      READ(NI,10)DESC,         (ARR(I),RVEC(I),I=1,9)
      READ(NI,11)ADESC,         ARR(10),RVEC(10)
   10 FORMAT(A7,1X, 9(A2,F6.4))
   11 FORMAT(A7,1X,A2,F6.4)
      WRITE(NO,20)DESC,(ARR(I),RVEC(I),I=1,10),SCALE
   20 FORMAT(1X,A7,1H ,10(A2,F6.4), * DATA IN E*,I2,* SCAL=*)
      RETURN
      END

      SUBROUTINE DEFLAT(FACTR,RIO)
C THIS ROUTINE DEFLATES THE I/O ARRAY TO ALTERNATE PERIOD
      DIMENSION RIO(10.10),FACTR(10)
      RETURN
      END

      SUBROUTINE BOATS
C CONSTRAIN POP NUMBERX IN INCOME GROUPS D,H, ANDI TO EFFECT MIGRATION
C OF THE WHITE POPULATION. FACTINC, AS INPUT, IS THE FACTOR THE GROUP IS
C TO BE REDUCED BY.
      DIMENSION ARRAY(9),SECTOR(10),GO(10),GROW(10)
      DIMENSION RIO(10,10), WP(9,10), WG(9,10), RN(9,10)
      DIMENSION DEPR(10), RITX(10), RINT(10), RIMP(10), RIMT(10)
      DIMENSION CONV(10,5), HSDN(9), YHSD(9), TAXS(9), SAVG(9)
      DIMENSION CONS(10,4), TRAF(9,4), RIMD(9), RDUT(9)
      DIMENSION RIMC(10), CAPF(10), COSV(10), CAPUT(10)
      DIMENSION PIMP(10), PWAG(10), PREN(10), PDEP(10), PINT(10)
      DIMENSION PTAX(10), CAPAC(10)
      DIMENSION CONST(10), FD(10), WAGES(9), RENTS(9), FACINF(9),YOLD(9)
      DIMENSION CONSIM(10), CONDEM(10), PRICE(10), SUBS(10), TOTCOV(9)
      DIMENSION EMPLOY(9,10)
```

177

```
      DIMENSION BASEGO(10)
      DIMENSION GOLD(10)
      DIMENSION REXP(10), RINV(10), STOC(10)
      DIMENSION FACTINC(9)
      COMMON/BLOCK1/ARRAY,SECTOR,GO,NYEAR,NI,NO,NBASE
      COMMON/BLOCK2/RIO,WP,WG,RN,DEPR,RITX,RINT,RIMP,RIMT           017
      COMMON/BLOCK3/CONV,HSDN,YHSD,TAXS,SAVG,CONS,TRAF,RIMD,RDUT    018
      COMMON/BLOCK4/RIMC,CAPF,COSV,CAPUT
      COMMON/BLOCK5/PIMP,PWAG,PREN,PDEP,PINT,PTAX
      CALL READV1(FACTINC)
      DO 120 I=1,9
      FACTINC(I)=1.-FACTINC(I)
      HSDN(I)=HSDN(I)*FACTINC(I)                                    020
  120 CONTINUE
      WRITE(NO,130)(ARRAY(I),I=1,4),(HSDN(I),I=1,4)
  130 FORMAT(/36H CONSTRAINED RURAL HOUSEHOLD NUMBERS/4(3X,A1,3X)/
     14F7.1/)
      WRITE(NO,140)(ARRAY(I),I=5,9),(HSDN(I),I=5,9)
  140 FORMAT(/36H CONSTRAINED URBAN HOUSEHOLD NUMBERS/5(3X,A1,3X)/
     15F7.1/)
      RETURN
      END

      SUBROUTINE AGCON(CONDEM)
C CONSTRAIN DEMAND ON MODAG SECTOR BY A GIVEN AMOUNT AND MOVE DIFFERENCE
C TODEMAND ON TRAD. CONSTR. AS INPUT, IS THE FACTOR MODAG IS TO BE
C REDUCED BY
      DIMENSION ARRAY(9),SECTOR(10),GO(10),GROW(10)
      DIMENSION RIO(10,10),WP(9,10),WG(9,10),RN(9,10)
      DIMENSION DEPR(10),RITX(10),RINT(10),RIMP(10), RIMT(10)
      DIMENSION CONV(10,5),HSDN(9), YHSD(9), TAXS(9), SAVG(9)
      DIMENSION CONS(10,4),TRAF(9,4),RIMD(9),RDUT(9)
      DIMENSION RIMC(10),CAPF(10), COSV(10), CAPUT(10)
      DIMENSION PIMP(10), PWAG(10), PREN(10), PDEP(10), PINT(10)
      DIMENSION PTAX(10), CAPAC(10)
      DIMENSION CONST(10), FD(10), WAGES(9), RENTS(9), FACTNF(9),YOLD(9)
      DIMENSION CONSIM(10), CONDEM(10), PRICE(10), SUBS(10), TOTCOV(9)
      DIMENSION EMPLOY(9,10)
      DIMENSION BASEGO(10)
      DIMENSION GOLD(10)
      DIMENSION REXP(10), RINV(10), STOC(10)
      DIMENSION CONSTR(10),DIF(10)
```

```
      COMMON/BLOCK1/ARRAY,SECTOR,GO,NYEAR,NI,NO,NBASE
      COMMON/BLOCK2/RIO,WP,WG,RN,DEPR,RITX,RINT,RIMP,RIMT          017
      COMMON/BLOCK3/CONV,HSDN,YHSD,TAXS,SAVG,CONS,TRAF,RIMD,RDUT   018
      COMMON/BLOCK4/RIMC,CAPF,COSV,CAPUT
      COMMON/BLOCK5/PIMP,PWAG,PREN,PDEP,PINT,PTAX                  020
      CALL READV5(CONSTR)
      DO 210 I=1,10
      CONSTR(I)=1.-CONSTR(I)
      DIF(I)=CONDEM(I)-CONDEM(I)*CONSTR(I)
      CONDEM(I)=CONDEM(I)-DIF(I)
  210 CONTINUE
      CONDEM(1)=CONDEM(1)+DIF(2)
      WRITE(NO,160)NYEAR,SECTOR,CONDEM
  160 FORMAT(I5,33H CONSTRAINED DEMAND ON 10 SECTORS/10(3X,A6)/10F9.0/)
      RETURN
      END
```

179

Index

DATE DUE

~~FEB 2 0 1980~~	
~~DEC 0 5 1992~~	
~~1993~~	

MP 728